AMERICAN THINK

STUDENT'S BOOK STARTER

Herbert Puchta, Jeff Stranks & Peter Lewis-Jones

CAMBRIDGE
UNIVERSITY PRESS

CONTENTS

PRONUNCIATION	THINK	SKILLS	
/h/ or /w/ in question words	**Values:** The Olympic Spirit **Self-esteem:** The "Me" flag	Reading	Website: Crazy about the Olympics Dialogue: Favorite soccer teams Photostory: Just a little joke
		Listening	Radio quiz: The One-Minute Challenge
		Writing	Completing a questionnaire: Personal information
Vowel sounds: adjectives	**Values:** Welcoming a new classmate **Train to Think:** Categorizing	Reading	Text messages: Hi there! Dialogue: Deciding what to do Culture: Masks from around the world
		Listening	Dialogues: Talking about feelings
		Writing	Text messages: Describing feelings and things
this / that / these / those	**Values:** Families **Self-esteem:** Being part of a family	Reading	Article: Kate Middleton Dialogue: Alicia's family Photostory: A song for Ruby
		Listening	Dialogues: Describing family
		Writing	Description: Your favorite room
Word stress in numbers	**Values:** My town/city **Train to Think:** Exploring numbers	Reading	Article: Window of the World Dialogues: In the stores Culture: Parks around the world
		Listening	Dialogues: Asking for directions
		Writing	A brochure for your town
Simple present verbs: third person	**Values:** Better together or better alone? **Self-esteem:** What makes you happy?	Reading	Newsletter: I love Glee Club! Quiz: Does TV control your life? Photostory: The school play
		Listening	Monologues: Describing electronic gadgets
		Writing	Paragraph: Days in your life
The /eɪ/ vowel sound	**Values:** Helping a friend **Train to Think:** Attention to detail	Reading	Article: A real friend Dialogue: A surprise for Olivia Culture: Welcoming people around the world
		Listening	Interview: Friendship bands
		Writing	Paragraph: Describing a friend

WELCOME

The alphabet

Aa Bb Cc Dd

Ee Ff Gg Hh

Ii Jj Kk Ll

Mm Nn Oo

Pp Qq Rr Ss

Tt Uu Vv Ww

Xx Yy Zz

1 🔊 1.02 Listen to the alphabet. Then listen again and repeat.

2 🔊 1.03 Listen to the sounds and repeat.

/eɪ/	/i/	/e/	/aɪ/	/oʊ/	/u/	/ɑr/
a h j k	b c d e g p t v z	f l m n s x	i y	o	q u w	r

3 SPEAKING Work in pairs. Spell your name to your partner. Your partner writes your name. Is he/she correct?

Colors

1 Write the colors in the correct places in the key.

black | blue | brown | green | gray | orange
pink | purple | red | white | yellow

Key

1 *white*   7 _____

2 _____   8 _____

3 _____   9 _____

4 _____   10 _____

5 _____   11 _____

6 _____

2 SPEAKING Work in pairs. What colors can you see around you? Tell your partner.

A

B

C *1*

D

E

F

G

H

I

J

K

L

M

N

O

P

International words

1 Match the words in the list with the photos. Write 1–16 in the boxes.

1 airport | 2 bus | 3 café
4 city | 5 banana | 6 hamburger
7 hotel | 8 phone | 9 pizza
10 restaurant | 11 sandwich
12 sushi | 13 taxi | 14 television
15 tablet | 16 wi-fi

2 ◀ 1.04 Listen, check, and repeat.

3 SPEAKING Work in pairs. Choose one of the words in Exercise 1 and spell it to your partner. He/She writes the word. Is he/she correct?

Articles: *a* and *an*

1 Match the sentences in the list with the pictures. Write 1–4 in the boxes.

1 It's a blue taxi.

2 It's an orange taxi.

3 It's a red taxi.

4 It's a black and white taxi.

2 Write *a* or *an*.

0 _____an_____ airport

1 _____ hotel

2 _____ red bus

3 _____ sandwich

4 _____ yellow taxi

5 _____ orange phone

6 _____ American restaurant

7 _____ wet umbrella

The day

Write the words in the list under the pictures.

afternoon | ~~evening~~ | morning | night

_____evening_____

_____

_____

_____

Saying *Hello* and *Goodbye*

🔊 1.05 **Complete the dialogues with the words in the list. Listen and check.**

Bye | Good | have | Hi | How | morning
night | See you | thanks | ~~this~~

1

ANDY   Hello. My name's Andy.

TOM   Hi, Andy. I'm Tom, and ⁰ *this* is Lucy.

LUCY   ¹_____ , Andy.

ANDY   Hi, Tom. Hi, Lucy.

2

ABI   ²_____ afternoon, Mrs. Hall.

MRS. HALL   Hi, Abi. ³_____ are you?

ABI   Great, ⁴_____ . And you?

MRS. HALL   I'm fine, thanks.

3

DARIUS   Good ⁵_____ , Mr. Thomas.

MR. THOMAS   Hello, Darius. How are you?

DARIUS   I'm fine, thank you.

MR. THOMAS   Good. I'll see you in class.

DARIUS   ⁶_____ , Mr. Thomas.

4

JIM   Bye, Rachel.

RACHEL   Bye, Jim. ⁷_____ later.

JIM   Yeah, ⁸_____ a good day.

5

SUE   Good ⁹_____ , Mom.

MOM   Night, Sue. Sleep well.

Classroom objects

1 Look at the pictures. Do you know these words? If not, ask your teacher: *What's ... in English?*

0 ___*door*___   1 _____

2 _____   3 _____

4 _____   5 _____

6 _____   7 _____

8 _____   9 _____

2 🔊 1.06 Write the words in the list under the pictures in Exercise 1. Listen, check, and repeat.

board | book | chair | computer | desk
~~door~~ | pen | pencil | projector | window

3 What other classroom objects can you think of?

4 SPEAKING Work in pairs. Ask and answer questions about the pictures in Exercise 1.

> *What's ... in English?*   *It's a desk.*

5 SPEAKING Work in pairs. Find things in your classroom and say the colors.

> *a red pen*   *an orange chair*

Numbers 0–20

1 🔊 1.07 Look at the numbers 0–20. Listen and repeat.

0	zero/"oh"	11	eleven
1	one	12	twelve
2	two	13	thirteen
3	three	14	fourteen
4	four	15	fifteen
5	five	16	sixteen
6	six	17	seventeen
7	seven	18	eighteen
8	eight	19	nineteen
9	nine	20	twenty
10	ten		

2 SPEAKING Work in pairs. Choose three numbers from Exercise 1. Tell a partner to write them. Is he/she correct?

3 🔊 1.08 Listen and write the phone numbers you hear.

1 _____   3 _____

2 _____   4 _____

Plural nouns

1 Write the words under the pictures.

0 ___*two chairs*___   1 _____   2 _____

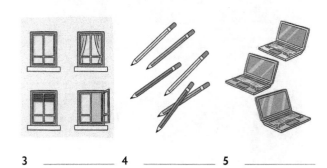

3 _____   4 _____   5 _____

2 Match the singular and plural nouns.

Singular		Plural	
0	one man	*b*	a	three people
1	one woman		b	four men
2	a person		c	six children
3	a child		d	five women

Classroom language

1 🔊 1.09 **Listen and number the phrases in the order you hear them. Write 1–10 in the boxes.**

2 🔊 1.10 **Listen again and say the phrases.**

☐ **a** Open your books.

☐ **b** Listen!

☐ **c** Raise your hand.

☐ **d** Look at the picture.

☐ **e** What does this mean?

☐ **f** Sorry, I don't understand.

☐ **g** That's right.

☐ **h** That's wrong.

1 **i** Close your books.

☐ **j** Work with a partner.

Numbers 20–100

1 🔊 1.11 **Match the numbers with the words. Listen and check.**

a	20			1	fifty
b	30			2	eighty
c	40			3	ninety
d	50			4	seventy
e	60			5	one hundred
f	70			6	thirty
g	80		*a*	7	twenty
h	90			8	sixty
i	100			9	forty

> **LOOK!**
> 33 = thirty-three   56 = fifty-six   97 = ninety-seven

2 🔊 1.12 **How do you say these numbers? Listen, check, and repeat.**

1	24	4	49	7	71
2	87	5	54	8	95
3	33	6	62		

3 **Write the numbers.**

0	24	*twenty-four*
1	47	_____
2	60	_____
3	89	_____
4	30	_____
5	58	_____
6	72	_____
7	91	_____

Messages

1 🔊 1.13 **Read and listen to the message. Complete the message to Luis.**

Hi, Luis,

Message from Brian Holmes.

His apartment number is ¹_____.

The bus number is ²_____.

His phone number is

³_____.

2 🔊 1.14 **Now listen and complete the message to Amy.**

Hi, Amy,

Message from Mrs. Davis.

Her address is ¹_____ Elm Street.

The bus number is ²_____.

Her telephone number is

³_____.

Review

1 🔊 1.15 **Work in groups. Play the first letter game.**

- Listen to the letter of the alphabet.
- How many examples can you find for each category in the table?
- You get one point for each correct answer. The winner is the group with the most points.

	0 _P_	1 ___	2 ___	3 ___	4 ___	5 ___
Color	*pink* *purple*					
Actor	*Sean Penn* *Al Pacino*					
Classroom object	*pencil* *projector*					
Number (0–20)	*—*					
International word	*pizza* *phone*					
Total Points	*9*					

2 **Complete the words with the missing vowels and then write them in the correct column in the table below.**

0 b _a_ n _a_ n _a_   6 ch _ _ _ r
1 d _ _ _ r   7 f _ v _
2 r _ st _ _ r _ nt   8 y _ ll _ w
3 _ r _ ng _   9 _ _ rp _ rt
4 p _ n   10 gr _ _ _ n
5 n _ n _   11 _ _ _ ght

International words	Colors	Numbers	Classroom objects
banana	___	___	___
___	___	___	___
___	___	___	___

3 SPEAKING **Work in pairs. Choose three pictures and spell the words for your partner to write. Is he/she correct?**

4 **Put the dialogues in order. Write 1–4 and 1–3 in the boxes.**

1

☐	JIM	Great, thanks. And you?
1	JIM	Good morning, Jack.
☐	JACK	I'm fine, thanks.
☐	JACK	Hi, Jim. How are you?

2

☐	LUCY	Yeah, have a good day.
☐	LUCY	Bye, Sara.
☐	SARA	Bye, Lucy. See you later.

1 | ONE WORLD

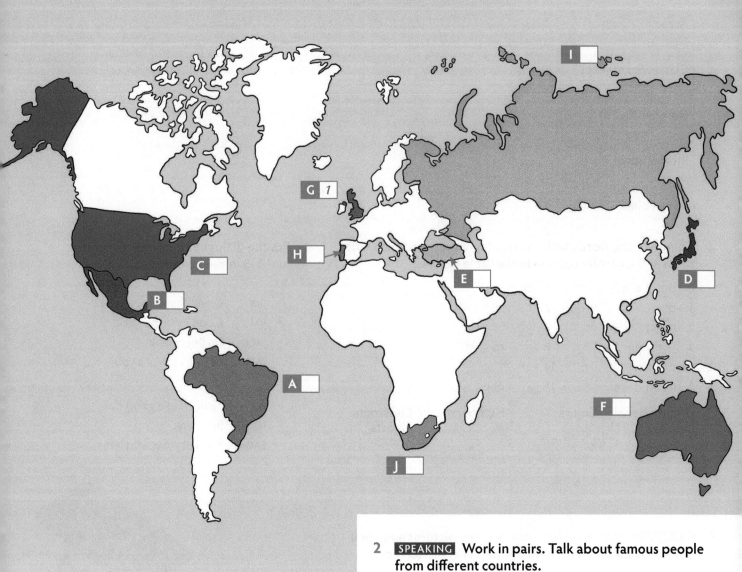

2 **SPEAKING** Work in pairs. Talk about famous people from different countries.

Neymar is from Brazil.

READING

1 Match the names of the countries with the places on the map. Write 1–10 in the boxes.

1	the U.K.	6	Brazil
2	Mexico	7	Portugal
3	the U.S.	8	Japan
4	Australia	9	Turkey
5	Russia	10	South Africa

3 ◀⟩ 1.16 Read and listen to the website and choose the correct words.

0 Pedro is from *Brazil* / *the U.S.*

1 Pedro is *10 / 11*.

2 Brittany is from *Manchester / London*.

3 Missy Franklin is a *swimmer / runner*.

4 Oleg is *Russian / Portuguese*.

5 Oleg is *11 / 12*.

6 Yumi is from *Japan / the U.K.*

7 Zheng Jie is a *runner / tennis player*.

Crazy about the Olympics

HOME · ABOUT · NEWS · CONTACT

Tell us about your Olympic favorites!

What's your name?
Pedro.

Where are you from?
I'm Brazilian. I'm from a city called Belo Horizonte.

How old are you?
I'm 10.

Who's your favorite sportsperson?
Usain Bolt.

Why is he/she your favorite sportsperson?
Because he's amazing!

What's your name?
My name is Brittany.

Where are you from?
I'm British. I'm from Manchester.

How old are you?
I'm 12.

Who's your favorite sportsperson?
My favorite sportsperson is Missy Franklin. She's a swimmer.

Why is he/she your favorite sportsperson?
Because she's great!

What's your name?
I'm Oleg.

Where are you from?
I'm from Russia. I live in Moscow.

How old are you?
I'm 11.

Who's your favorite sportsperson?
Mariya Savinova. She's a runner.

Why is he/she your favorite sportsperson?
Because she's fast!

What's your name?
My name is Yumi.

Where are you from?
I'm Japanese. I'm from Kyoto.

How old are you?
I'm 11.

Who's your favorite sportsperson?
Zheng Jie. She's a tennis player from China.

Why is he/she your favorite sportsperson?
Because she's awesome!

■ THiNK VALUES ■

The Olympic Spirit

Answer the questions in the website for yourself. Write your answers. Tell a partner.

What's your name? _____

Where are you from? _____

How old are you? _____

Who is your favorite sportsperson?

_____

Why is he/she your favorite?

_____

VOCABULARY
Countries and nationalities

1 🔊 1.17 **Write the country under the flag. Listen and check.**

Australia | Brazil | Japan | Mexico | Portugal | ~~Russia~~ | South Africa | the U.K. | the U.S. | Turkey

0 _Russia_   1 _____   2 _____   3 _____   4 _____

5 _____   6 _____   7 _____   8 _____   9 _____

2 **Look at Exercise 1. Complete the table with the nationalities of the countries.**

-an	-ish	-ese
Russian		

3 **SPEAKING** **Work in pairs. Describe a flag to your partner. Which country is it from?**

> This flag is white, blue, and red.

> Is it the Russian flag?

> Yes, it is!

Workbook page 12 ➡

GRAMMAR
Question words

1 **Look at the website on page 13 and complete the questions with the words in the list. Then circle the correct words to complete the rule.**

How | ~~What~~ | Where | Who | Why

0 _What_ 's your name?
1 _____ are you from?
2 _____ old are you?
3 _____ 's your favorite sportsperson?
4 _____ is he/she your favorite sportsperson?

> **RULE:** *How*, *What*, *Where*, *Who*, and *Why* are [1]question / because words.
> We often use the word [2]question / because to answer a **Why** question.

2 **Choose the correct words.**

0 (How)/ Why old is your best friend?
1 *What / Where* is your mother from?
2 *How's / What's* your favorite color?
3 *Where / Who* is your favorite singer?
4 *Why / Where* is he/she your favorite singer?

3 **SPEAKING** **Work in pairs. Ask and answer the questions in Exercises 1 and 2.**

> What's your name?

> My name is Belena.

Workbook page 10 ➡

Pronunciation
/h/ or /w/ in question words
Go to page 120. 🔊

14

LISTENING

1 Work in pairs. Look at the photos and check (✓) the correct flag for each photo.

2 🔊1.20 Listen to a radio quiz called *The One-Minute Challenge* and check your answers.

GRAMMAR

The verb *be*

1 Match sentences a–h with items 1–4. Write the letters in the boxes.

1 Bruno Mars | e | |
2 Maria Sharapova
3 sushi
4 cariocas

a She's Russian.
b It's Japanese.
c They're Brazilian.
d It's food.
e He's a singer.
f They're from Rio de Janeiro.
g She's a tennis player.
h He's American.

2 Look at the sentences from the radio quiz. Choose the correct words. Then complete the rule.

1 I *am / are* from London.
2 You *am / are* wrong.
3 They *am / are* from Rio de Janeiro in Brazil.

> **RULE:** The verb *be* changes for different subject pronouns.
> I *am* American.
> You/We/They [1]_____ American.
> He/She/It [2]_____ American.
> We often use contracted forms after pronouns.
> I am = I'm
> You/We/They are = You're / We're / They're
> He/She/It is = He's / She's / It's

> **LOOK!**
>
> | Singular | Plural |
> |---|---|
> | I | we |
> | you | you |
> | he/she/it | they |

3 Complete the sentences. Use contracted forms where possible.

0 I _'m_ from New York.
1 She _____ a famous actor.
2 Jacob _____ from the U.S.
3 Lucas and Ben _____ my best friends.
4 We _____ in English class.
5 You _____ wrong. Sorry.

Workbook page 11

■ THiNK SELF-ESTEEM ■

My flag

1 Choose things that are important to you.

● two colors   ● one animal
● two activities

2 **SPEAKING** Use your ideas from Exercise 1 to draw your flag. Tell your partner about it.

My flag is blue and red. They're my favorite colors. Here is a soccer ball. It's my favorite sport. Here is music. I love music. Here is a panda. It's my favorite animal.

READING

1 🔊 1.21 **Read and listen to the dialogue. Who knows more about soccer, Jamie or Marta?**

JAMIE	Nice shirt.
MARTA	Thank you. It's the new Barcelona shirt.
JAMIE	I know. I'm a Barcelona fan, too. So what's your name?
MARTA	Marta. And what's your name?
JAMIE	I'm Jamie.
MARTA	Nice to meet you, Jamie.
JAMIE	Nice to meet you, too. Where are you from, Marta?
MARTA	I'm from Spain. I'm from a small town called Teruel.
JAMIE	Spain is a beautiful country.
MARTA	Yes, it is. So who's your favorite Barcelona player?
JAMIE	Umm … Lucas Silva.
MARTA	The Brazilian player?
JAMIE	Yes, he's great.
MARTA	Yes, he is. But he isn't a Barcelona player.
JAMIE	No?
MARTA	He's a Real Madrid player.
JAMIE	Oh!
MARTA	It's late. Time to go. Bye, Jamie.
JAMIE	OK, bye.

2 **Mark the sentences T (true) or F (false). Write the correct sentences in your notebook.**

0   Jamie is a Real Madrid fan. | F |
    Jamie is a Barcelona fan.
1   Marta is Spanish.
2   Marta is from a big town.
3   Lucas Silva is Italian.
4   Lucas Silva is a Barcelona player.

3 **Write the questions.**

1   Q _____
    A   I'm Jamie.
2   Q _____
    A   I'm from a small town called Teruel.
3   Q _____
    A   Lucas Silva.

FUNCTIONS
Getting to know someone

1 🔊 1.22 **Put the dialogue in order. Listen and check.**

	GINA	Nice to meet you, too.
	GINA	I'm from San Francisco.
	GINA	Yes, it is.
	GINA	I'm Gina.
1	GINA	What's your name?
	PAOLO	Nice to meet you, Gina.
	PAOLO	Where are you from, Gina?
	PAOLO	San Francisco is a beautiful city.
	PAOLO	I'm Paolo. And you?

2 **SPEAKING Work in pairs. Act out the dialogue.**

3 **SPEAKING Work in pairs. Make your own dialogue.**

VOCABULARY
Adjectives

1 🔊 1.23 **Write the words in the list under the pictures. Listen and check.**

a big TV | a dirty bike | a fast car | a new pen
a slow bus | a small pizza | an expensive computer
an old phone | cheap tickets | clean shirts

0 ___a big TV___

1 _____

2 _____

3 _____

4 _____

5 _____

6 _____

7 _____

8 _____

9 _____

2 **Match the opposites.**

0	new	d		a	slow
1	big			b	expensive
2	dirty			c	small
3	cheap			d	old
4	fast			e	clean

3 **Put the words in order.**

0 old / computer / an _____an old computer_____
1 a / bike / new _____
2 expensive / an / hotel _____
3 train / fast / a _____
4 dirty / shoes _____
5 book / cheap / a _____

> **LOOK!** In English adjectives always stay the same.
> *new pens* **NOT** *news pens*
> *green cars* **NOT** *greens cars*

Workbook page 13 ➤

WRITING
Personal information

Look at the questionnaire. Answer the questions about you in full sentences.

The New York English
Summer Camp

We're really excited about your visit next month.

Answer the questions about yourself to find the perfect roommate.

What's your name?

_____

Where are you from?

_____

How old are you?

_____

Who's your favorite singer?

_____

What's your favorite color?

_____

Just a little joke

1 **Look at the photos and answer the questions.**

1 There are three friends in photo 1. What are their names?

2 Who's the other boy?

3 Where is he from?

2 ◀)) 1.24 **Now read and listen to the photostory. Check your answers.**

RUBY Hi, Ellie.
ELLIE Hi, Ruby. How's it going?
RUBY Great, thanks. Oh, hello, Dan.
DAN Hi, you two.

1

RUBY Who's that?
DAN That's *Thomas*.
ELLIE Who's he?
DAN He's in my class. He's new.

2

ELLIE Where's he from?
DAN He's from Paris. He's cool. Oh, time to go now. See you tomorrow.
RUBY Bye, Dan.
ELLIE See you later.

3

ELLIE He's from Paris?
RUBY Paris. That is so awesome!
ELLIE I know!

4

DEVELOPING SPEAKING

3 ◖◀ EP1 **Watch to find out how the story continues.**

1 Is Thomas from France?

2 Where is he from?

4 ◖◀ EP1 **Watch again. Choose the correct word in each sentence.**

0 They are in (an ice cream shop) / a fast food restaurant.

1 The chocolate ice cream is for *Ellie / Ruby.*

2 Thomas is *American / French.*

3 He's from *Paris, Texas / Paris, France.*

4 The ice cream's *very good / not very good.*

PHRASES FOR FLUENCY

1 **Find the expressions 1–4 in the story. Who says them?**

1 How's it going? _____

2 See you later. _____

3 That is so awesome! _____

4 I know! _____

2 **How do you say the expressions in Exercise 1 in your language?**

3 **Change the underlined expressions. Use an expression from Exercise 1.**

1 A This is my new bicycle.

 B Great! _____

2 Hi, Jorge. How are you? _____

3 A This is a nice computer.

 B Yes, it is. _____

4 OK, time to go. Goodbye! _____

4 **Complete the mini-dialogues with the expressions from Exercise 1.**

0 A This concert is great!

 B *I know* _____ !

1 A Hello, Ben!

 B _____ ?

2 A Look at my new phone.

 B _____ !

3 A Goodbye, Mike.

 B _____, Annie.

FUNCTIONS
Talking about yourself and others

1 **Match the questions and answers.**

0 Who's that? ___b___

1 Where's he from? ☐

2 How old are you? ☐

3 Who's your favorite singer? ☐

a He's from Paris.

b That's Thomas.

c Beyoncé.

d I'm 11.

2 **Put the words in the correct order to make dialogues.**

1 A that / who's / ?

 Who's that? _____

 B Mary / that's

 _____

 A she / from / where's / ?

 _____

 B the U.K. / from / she's

 _____

2 A they / are / who / ?

 _____

 B Mario / are / and / they / Alex

 _____

 A are / from / where / they / ?

 _____

 B from / they / Mexico / are

 _____

3 A Hi, / your / name / what's / ?

 _____

 B Rob / I'm

 _____

 A old / you, / how / are / Rob / ?

 _____

 B 12 / I'm

 _____

 A favorite / your / singer / who's / ?

 _____

 B Ed Sheeran.

3 SPEAKING **Work in pairs. Act out the dialogues. Then make similar dialogues.**

2 I FEEL HAPPY

READING

1 Match the phrases with the photos. Write 1–6 in the boxes.

1	on a train	4	at school
2	on a plane	5	on a beach
3	at a stadium	6	on a bus

2 **SPEAKING** Work in pairs. Student A, close your book. Student B, test your partner.

What's A?   *It's on a beach.*

3 🔊 1.25 **Read and listen to the text messages on page 21. Where are the people? Write the names under the correct photos in Exercise 1.**

4 **Mark the sentences T (true) or F (false).**

0	Nicky is worried.	T
1	Andrea is at school.	
2	Andrea, Amy, and Katie are on vacation.	
3	Ryan is not happy.	
4	The bus driver isn't angry.	
5	James is at a baseball game.	

A

B

C

D

E 1

F

Hi there!

Nicky

Hi there, I'm at school. There are 12 girls and 15 boys in my new class. They aren't very friendly. I'm a little worried. 😟 But the teacher's really cool. How are you? Are you OK? See you soon.

Tuesday, 10:06 a.m.

Andrea

Look at my photo. I'm on the beach. It's hot and sunny. I'm very happy. 😊 I'm with 2 American girls, Amy and Katie. It's fun! What about you? How's your vacation? Is it nice there?

Sunday, 3:26 p.m.

Ryan

I'm on the bus to school and I'm not very happy. It's so full and I'm very hot. 😣 The driver isn't very nice and he's angry. Ten more minutes to get to school. See you soon!

Monday, 8:16 a.m.

James

Hi, I'm at the baseball stadium. The score's 4-0 for the other team. The players on my team aren't good. Are they tired or bored? Baseball is a great sport, but this game isn't great. Bye!

Saturday, 4:58 p.m.

■ THiNK VALUES ■

Welcoming a new classmate

1 **Look at the picture and answer the questions.**

1 Where is Emily?
2 How is she?
3 Why isn't Emily happy?

The first day at my new school. I'm worried and I'm sad. Where are my friends?

2 **Imagine you are Emily's classmate. What's OK 🙂 or not OK 🙁?**

0 talk to Emily   🙂 _____

1 help Emily _____
2 smile at Emily _____
3 laugh at Emily _____
4 not talk to Emily _____
5 ask Emily questions _____

3 **SPEAKING** **Compare your ideas with a partner.**

It's OK to smile at Emily.

It isn't OK to …

4 **SPEAKING** **Work in pairs. Think of other things you can do to help Emily on her first day.**

VOCABULARY
Adjectives to describe feelings

1 🔊 1.26 **Match the feelings in the list with the pictures. Write 1–10 in the boxes. Listen and check.**

1 angry | 2 bored | 3 cold | 4 excited
5 hot | 6 hungry | 7 sad | 8 thirsty
9 tired | 10 worried

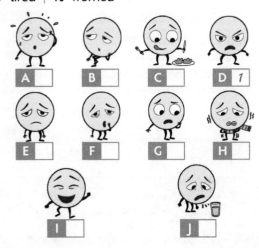

2 **Match the sentences with the pictures. Write 1–6 in the boxes.**

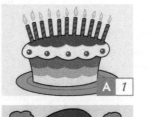

1 It's your birthday.
2 It's one o'clock in the morning.
3 There's a great movie on TV, but the TV is broken.
4 The weather is terrible!
5 Your mom is angry with you.
6 You're on a plane.

3 **SPEAKING Work in pairs. Tell your partner how you feel in the situations in Exercise 2.**

Number 1: I'm excited.   *Number 2: I'm ...*

Workbook page 21

GRAMMAR
be (negative: singular and plural)

1 **Look at the text messages on page 21. Complete the sentences. Then complete the rule.**

1 They _____ very friendly.
2 The driver _____ very nice, and he's angry.

> **RULE:** We form the negative of *be* with subject + *be* +
> ¹ _____ .
>
> *I'm not* sad. (**am not**)
> *You* **aren't** sad. (**are not**)
> *He/She/It* ² _____ sad. (**is not**)
> *We* **aren't** sad. (**are not**)
> *They* ³ _____ sad. (**are not**)

2 **Complete the sentences with the correct negative form of the verb *be*.**

0 Madison _*isn't*_ happy today. She's very sad.
1 You _____ on my team. You're on Mike's team.
2 They _____ eleven years old. They're ten.
3 No pizza for me, thanks. I _____ hungry.
4 Lucia's favorite color is blue. It _____ green.

3 **Complete the sentences with the correct form of the verb *be*.**

0 We _'re_ ✓ Mexican. We _aren't_ ✗ American.
1 I _____ ✗ sad. I _____ ✓ happy!
2 Danny _____ ✓ twelve. He _____ ✗ eleven.
3 It _____ ✗ hot. It _____ ✓ cold!
4 Lucy _____ ✓ worried. She _____ ✗ excited.

Workbook page 18

> ### Pronunciation
> Vowel sounds: adjectives
> **Go to page 120.** 🔊

■ TRAIN TO THiNK ■
Categorizing

1 **Read the words in the list. Put them into four categories. There are four words for each category.**

afternoon | angry | book | bored | chair | desk
evening | excited | gray | morning | night
orange | pencil | purple | white | worried

2 **SPEAKING Work in pairs. Read your categories out loud. Compare them.**

Category 1 - gray, orange, ...

LISTENING

1 🔊 1.29 **Listen to four dialogues. Match two with the pictures. Write a number in the boxes.**

2 🔊 1.29 **Listen again. Complete the dialogues with** *cold*, *tired*, *excited*, **and** *angry*.

1 A Is Noah's mom sad?
  B No, she isn't. She's _____ .

2 A Are Chris and David worried?
  B No, they aren't. They're _____ .

3 A Is Ted worried?
  B No, he isn't. He's _____ .

4 A Is Ashley hot?
  B No, she isn't. She's very _____ .

GRAMMAR

be (questions and short answers)

1 **Look at picture A in Exercise 1. Choose the correct answer. Then complete the rule and the table.**

A Are you hot, Ashley?
B *Yes, I am. / No, I'm not.*

> **RULE:** We form questions with [1]_____ + subject.
> We form short answers with [2]_____ + subject + *be* (+ *not*).

Question	Short affirmative answer	Short negative answer
Am I in your class?	Yes, you **are**.	No, you **aren't**.
Are you OK?	Yes, I **am**.	No, I **'m not**.
[1]_____ he/she/it here?	Yes, he/she/it **is**.	No, he/she/it [4]_____ .
Are we on this team?	Yes, we **are**.	No, we **aren't**.
[2]_____ they OK?	Yes, they [3]_____ .	No, they [5]_____ .

2 **Put the words in order to make questions. Write the answers.**

0 African / he / Is / South / ? (yes)
  Is he South African?   *Yes, he is.*

1 hungry / you / Are / ? (no)
  _____   _____

2 Brazil / they / from / Are / ? (yes)
  _____   _____

3 she / Is / tired / ? (no)
  _____   _____

4 late / I / Am / ? (no)
  _____   _____

A ☐

B ☐

3 **Look at the rule again. Complete the dialogues.**

1 A ___Are___ you angry, Grace?
  B No, I _____ . I'm just tired.

2 A _____ Chris and Tim your best friends?
  B Yes, they _____ . They _____ in my class at school.

3 A _____ Ms. Brown your English teacher?
  B No, she _____ . She's my mother's friend.

4 A Am I in your class?
  B No, you _____ . You _____ in Joe's class.

5 A _____ Juan Mexican?
  B _____ . He's from Merida.

6 A _____ we late?
  B _____ . We're early.

4 SPEAKING **Work in pairs. Ask and answer.**

Is soccer your favorite sport?

Are you cold?

Are your best friends from the U.S.?

Is your teacher in the classroom?

5 SPEAKING **Think of three more questions to ask your partner. Then ask and answer.**

Workbook page 18 ➤

READING

1 Read the dialogue and choose the correct option.

Nick and Ethan decide to …

a   go to the movie theater.

b   listen to music.

c   go to a club for young people.

2 🔊 1.30 **Read the dialogue again and listen. Number the photos in the order that Ethan talks about them. Write 1–5 in the boxes.**

ETHAN	What's wrong, Nick? Are you tired?
NICK	Tired? No, I'm not tired. I'm bored.
ETHAN	Why are you bored?
NICK	Because there's nothing to do. Nothing at all.
ETHAN	Well, there's a baseball game at five. It's on TV.
NICK	Baseball? I don't like it.
ETHAN	Really? What about a movie? There's a great new movie on at the movie theater downtown.
NICK	A movie? Who's in it?
ETHAN	Ben Stiller. He's so funny.
NICK	Ben Stiller? I don't like him. He's not funny. He's terrible.
ETHAN	Well, how about some music? Listen to this song. It's the new one from Maroon 5.
NICK	Maroon 5? Are you kidding? I don't like them.
ETHAN	Well, do you like ice cream? The new ice cream shop is open in the mall.
NICK	Ice cream? No, I don't like it.
ETHAN	What! You don't like ice cream?
NICK	No, I don't.
ETHAN	OK, how about the club?
NICK	What club?
ETHAN	The new youth club, you know, for teenagers.
NICK	Hmm, I'm not sure.
ETHAN	But Jen is a member.
NICK	Jen?
ETHAN	Yes, Jen Carter.
NICK	Jen Carter?
ETHAN	Yes, she goes there every Friday.
NICK	Really? Let's go!

3 Correct the sentences. Write the correct sentences in your notebook.

0   Nick is tired.
    He isn't tired. He's bored.

1   The baseball game is at eight.

2   Johnny Depp is in the movie.

3   The song is by The Feeling.

4   The new ice cream shop is at the beach.

5   Nick is a member of the new youth club.

A

B

C

D   1

E

GRAMMAR
Object pronouns

1 **Complete the dialogues with *them*, *it*, and *him*. Read the dialogue on page 24 again and check. Then use the words to complete the table.**

| ETHAN | There's a baseball game at five. |
| NICK | Baseball? I don't like [1]_____ . |

| ETHAN | Ben Stiller is so funny. |
| NICK | I don't like [2]_____ . |

| ETHAN | Listen to this song. |
| NICK | Maroon 5? I don't like [3]_____ . |

Subject	Object
I	me
you	you
he	[1]_____
she	her
it	[2]_____
we	us
they	[3]_____

2 **Complete the dialogues with the correct object pronouns.**

0 A Dad's angry.
  B Yes, he isn't very happy with ___us___ , Tom.
1 A Do you like Mumford & Sons?
  B No, I don't like _____ .
2 A Do you like Jennifer Lopez?
  B Yes, I like _____ . She's great.
3 A Do you like _____ ?
  B Yes, I think you and Peter are great.
4 A Do you like _____ ?
  B Yes, I think Jack is funny.
5 A Do you like my new bike?
  B Yes, I like _____ .
6 A Rob, I really like _____ .
  B I really like you too, Alice.

Workbook page 19

VOCABULARY
Positive and negative adjectives

1 **Look at the words in the list. Write N (negative) or P (positive) in the boxes.**

awful ☐ | bad ☐ | excellent ☐ | exciting ☐
funny ☐ | good ☐ | great ☐ | terrible ☐

2 **SPEAKING Work in pairs. Say one example for each of the following.**

> *How to Train Your Dragon 2 is a funny movie.*

a a funny movie
b an excellent actor
c a bad movie
d an exciting computer game
e a great sportsperson
f a terrible singer
g a great country
h a good book
i an awful actor

Workbook page 21

FUNCTIONS
Expressing likes and dislikes

1 **Which of these sentences means "it's good"? Which means "it's bad"?**

I don't like Taylor Swift.
I like Shakira.

2 **Put the words in the correct order to make questions.**

A you / like / Coldplay / do / ?
B you / Katy Perry / like / do / ?

3 **Match the answers to the questions in Exercise 2.**

1 No, I don't like them. They're terrible. ☐
2 Yes, I like her. She's great. ☐

4 **SPEAKING Work in pairs. Talk about the movies, actors, bands, and singers you really like and don't like.**

> *Do you like Lorde?*

> *Yes, I like her. I think she's great.*

> *Do you like the Divergent movies?*

> *No, I don't like them. They're terrible.*

Culture

Masks from around the world

1

This is a lion mask from China. In many countries in Asia, there are lion dances. There are always two people in a lion – the mask is on the head of one dancer. The lion dances are very beautiful. Tourists *love* them.

2

This mask is from North America. It's a mask from the First Nations people in Canada. The mask is for the medicine man.

3

The masks here are from Greece. They are 2,000 years old. They are masks for the actors in the Greek theater.

5

Masks are an important part of the carnival in Venice, Italy. There are many different types of carnival masks. For example, the mask in this picture is called the Colombina. Carnival masks are often very beautiful and some are very expensive.

4

These are Halloween masks. Halloween is on October 31. Children in many countries around the world, for example, in the U.S. and the U.K., wear Halloween masks. They go from house to house and say "Trick or treat." People give them candy ("treats").

1 **Look at the photos on page 26. Where can you see these things? Write 1–5 in the boxes.**

- [ ] a candy
- [ ] b tourists
- [ ] c a First Nations mask
- [ ] d a lion
- [ ] e a theater
- [ ] f a dancer

2 **What feelings can you see in the masks?**

> Mask number 1 is happy.

3 🔊 1.31 **Read and listen to the article. Which countries are the masks from?**

4 **Read the article again. Mark the sentences T (true) or F (false).**

- 0 The lion dance is from Canada. — F
- 1 The First Nations mask is for a doctor. ☐
- 2 The Greek masks are 200 years old. ☐
- 3 Halloween is a holiday only in the U.S. and the U.K. ☐
- 4 Colombina is a type of Italian mask. ☐

5 **SPEAKING** **Which of the masks do you like? Which do you not like? Why?**

WRITING
Describing feelings and things

1 **Read the text messages. Write the names under the photos.**

2 **Read the text messages again and answer the questions.**

1 Where is Henry?
2 Is he happy?
3 Why or why not?
4 Where is Tom?
5 Is he happy?
6 Why or why not?

3 **How do Tom and Henry …**

1 start their text?
2 finish their text?

4 **Imagine you want to write a text message to a friend. Think of answers to these questions.**

1 Where are you?
2 Are you happy?
3 Why or why not?

5 **Use your answers in Exercise 4 to write a text message (35–50 words) to a friend.**

Tom

Hi, Sarah. I'm at school. It's lunchtime and I'm really hungry. But I'm sad. The food at school today isn't good. I'm also cold. The sun isn't out. It's not a great day. What about you? Is your day good? Bye.

Today, 1:12 p.m.

Henry

Hi, Olivia. I'm in the car with my family. I'm excited because I'm on vacation. Yay! Two more hours to get to the beach! How are you? Are you OK? See you soon!

Today, 10:03 a.m.

A

B

READING AND WRITING
Part 3: Multiple-choice replies

1 Complete the five conversations. Choose the correct answer A, B, or C.

0 What's your name?
    A I'm 11.
    (B) It's Kylie.
    C Yes, I am.

1 How old are you?
    A I'm Brazilian.
    B I'm 12.
    C It's John.

2 Are we late?
    A Yes, we are.
    B No, I'm not.
    C Yes, he is.

3 Do you like Beyoncé?
    A No, I like her.
    B Yes, I am.
    C Yes, I like her.

4 Where are you from?
    A I'm 13.
    B Yes, I am.
    C Mexico.

5 Is Tom your friend?
    A Yes, we are.
    B Yes, he is.
    C Yes, I am.

Part 2: Multiple-choice sentence completion

2 Read the sentences about Jim. Choose the best word (A, B, or C) for each space.

0 Hi, my name _____ Jim.
    A am   **(B)** is   **C** are

1 It _____ my birthday today.
    A are   **B** am   **C** is

2 I _____ 12 years old.
    A am   **B** is   **C** are

3 I am _____ my school.
    A at   **B** on   **C** to

4 I like Ed Sheeran. He's a _____ singer.
    A great   **B** awful   **C** terrible

5 I _____ like sports.
    A aren't   **B** don't   **C** isn't

VOCABULARY

1 **Complete the sentences with the words in the list. There are two extra words.**

awful | Brazil | clean | excited | expensive | hot
hungry | old | Russian | the U.K. | British | thirsty

1 I want a sandwich. I'm _____ .
2 She's from Moscow. She's _____ .
3 Open the window, please. I'm _____ !
4 This pizza is _____ . I don't like it!
5 He's _____ . I think he's from Sheffield.
6 I'm 12 and my big brother Jack is 23. He's _____ !
7 Are you _____ ? OK, here's a glass of water.
8 It's $175? Oh, it's very _____ .
9 Brasilia is a big city in _____ .
10 We're on the train to Washington! We're very _____ !

/10

GRAMMAR

2 **Complete the sentences with the words in the list.**

don't | her | How | it | Where | Why

1 Mike and Annie aren't here. _____ are they?
2 This is my new shirt. I really like _____ .
3 She's my friend. I like _____ a lot.
4 _____ old are you?
5 I _____ like hamburgers.
6 A _____ are you here?
  B Because it's a nice place.

3 **Find and correct the mistake in each sentence.**

1 I not like sports.   _____
2 What old is your brother?   _____
3 Are the from Peru?   _____
4 It aren't an expensive computer.   _____
5 He's the new boy in the class. I like he. _____
6 What is your favorite singer?   _____

/12

FUNCTIONAL LANGUAGE

4 **Write the missing words.**

1 A Who _____ she?
  B She's Maria. She's _____ Mexico.
2 A _____ are they from?
  B Mexico. They _____ Mexican.
3 A _____ you like Taylor Swift?
  B Yes, I like her. She _____ a great singer.
4 A I _____ like this movie. It's awful!
  B Oh, really? I _____ it. It's funny!

/8

MY SCORE [ ] /30

| 22 – 30 |
| 10 – 21 |
| 0 – 9 |

A

B

C

D 1

READING

1 **Match the family members with the photos. Write 1–4 in the boxes.**

1 brother and sister
2 mother and son
3 father and daughter
4 husband and wife

2 SPEAKING **Think of famous examples of the following. Tell your partner.**

1 a husband and wife
2 a mother and daughter
3 a father and son
4 sisters
5 brothers

> *Brad Pitt and Angelina Jolie are a famous husband and wife.*

3 SPEAKING **Look at the photos on page 31. Use words from Exercise 1 to talk about them.**

4 ◀)) 1.32 **Read and listen to the article. Mark the sentences T (true) or F (false).**

0 Kate Middleton is from England. `T`
1 She has three brothers and sisters.
2 Kate's picture is never in the newspapers.
3 William's father is Prince Charles.
4 Kate's home is new.
5 Kate and William's apartment is small.

Kate Middleton

Kate Middleton is an English woman. She likes sports (especially field hockey) and photography. She's a very busy person. She works with many organizations to help children and sportspeople.

Kate's family is from Berkshire in England. She has a sister named Pippa and a brother named James.

So, is she a "normal" woman?

Not really. Now, she's famous all over the world. Her picture is often in the newspapers, and she's often on TV. She's The Duchess of Cambridge. Her husband is Prince William, the Duke of Cambridge. William's father is Prince Charles and his grandmother is Queen Elizabeth.

William and Kate have a son named George and a daughter named Charlotte. George was born in 2013, and Charlotte was born in 2015.

Kate and William's home is an apartment in Kensington Palace, in London. The palace is 300 years old. Their apartment is really big, with twenty bedrooms and three kitchens.

▰ THiNK VALUES ▰

Families

1 **Complete the sentences with at least one word from the list. Use a dictionary to help you.**

friendly | interested in … | patient
helpful | kind | strict | generous

1 A good brother/sister is _____ .
2 A good father is _____ .
3 A good mother is _____ .
4 A good grandfather/grandmother is _____ .

2 **SPEAKING** **Compare your ideas with others in the class.**

GRAMMAR
Possessive 's

1 **Look at the examples. Then complete the rule.**

1 Kate's family is from Berkshire in England.
2 William and Kate's apartment is in Kensington Palace.

> **RULE:** We talk about possession with noun + 's.
> Peter _____ sister = the sister of Peter

2 **Look at the photos and write the correct words with 's.**

my sister

0 _____ *my sister's phone* _____

Patrick

1 _____

Mrs. White

2 _____

my cousin

3 _____

Wendy

4 _____

my uncle

5 _____

> **LOOK!** We use **'s** for both possessives and contractions.
> *Tom's house is big.* (The house of Tom is big.)
> *She's my cousin.* (She is my cousin.)

Workbook page 28

VOCABULARY
Family members

1 🔊 1.33 **Complete Nicolás' family tree with the words in the list. Then listen and check.**

aunt | brother | cousin | father | grandfather
~~grandmother~~ | mother | sister | uncle

Maria — José
0 *grandmother* | 1 _____

Pablo | Susana | Jaime | Marta
2 _____ | 3 _____ | 4 _____ | 5 _____

Nicolás | Antonio | Ana | Sara
6 _____ | 7 _____ | 8 _____

2 **Look at the article on page 31. Complete the sentences with the words in the list.**

brother | ~~father~~ | grandfather | son | wife

0 William is George's ___ *father* ___ .
1 Kate is William's _____ .
2 George is Kate's _____ .
3 Prince Charles is George's _____ .
4 James is Kate and Pippa's _____ .

3 **SPEAKING Write three or four sentences about your family. Tell your partner.**

> *My uncle Antonio is my mother's brother.*

Workbook page 31

GRAMMAR
Possessive adjectives

1 **Look at the article on page 31. Complete the sentences and match them with the people. Then complete the table.**

1 _____ grandmother is Queen Elizabeth. ☐

2 _____ husband is Prince William. ☐

3 _____ apartment is really big. ☐

a William and Kate
b William
c Kate

Subject	Possessive adjectives
I	my
you	your
he	1 _____
she	2 _____
it	its
we	our
they	3 _____

2 **Complete the dialogue with words from Exercise 1.**

STEVE — Hello. ⁰ *My* name's Steve. What's ¹_____ name?

JANE — Hi. I'm Jane and this is Renata. She's Brazilian. She's here on vacation with ²_____ mother and father.

STEVE — Hi, Renata.

RENATA — Hi, Steve. How are you?

STEVE — Fine, thanks. So, you and ³_____ parents are from Brazil? Do you speak Spanish?

RENATA — No, we speak Portuguese. It's ⁴_____ first language.

JANE — Do you have any brothers or sisters?

RENATA — No, just me! And you?

JANE — Yes, I have two brothers. ⁵_____ names are Alex and Richard. They love soccer! And they love Brazilian soccer!

RENATA — Great! My father is a soccer fan, too – ⁶_____ favorite team is Flamengo.

Workbook page 28 ▶

LISTENING

1 🔊 1.34 **Listen to three people talking about their family. Write 1–3 in the boxes.**

2 🔊 1.34 **Listen again and complete the sentences. Write one word in each space.**

1 Jordan's family is very _____ . His uncle, Jack, is always very _____ .

2 Tania's _____ are in Australia. Her _____ , Clare, is nice, but sometimes she's difficult, too.

3 Manuel has _____ cousins. His cousin Monica is very _____ to her brothers, sisters, and friends.

■ THiNK SELF-ESTEEM ■
Being part of a family

1 **Complete the "ME" table. Write the names of four people in your family who are important to you and a word to describe them.**

ME

	Name	Adjective
1		
2		
3		
4		

PARTNER

	Name	Adjective
1		
2		
3		
4		

2 **SPEAKING Work in pairs. Ask your partner what he/she wrote. Write his/her answers in the "PARTNER" table.**

3 **SPEAKING Tell the class about …**

a your table.
b your partner's table.

READING

1 **Read the dialogue quickly and answer the questions.**

1 Where are the two girls?

2 Who is Debbie?

2 🔊 1.35 **Read the dialogue again and listen. Answer the questions.**

1 Who's in the photo?

2 Does Alicia like her brother Brian?

3 Are the books and magazines Brian's?

4 Are the DVDs Alicia's?

5 Does Brian like his sister?

ALICIA	So, ⁰ ___*this*___ is my bedroom. Do you like it?
DEBBIE	Yes! It's really nice. I like your bed. And the curtains are great!
ALICIA	Thank you. I like my room, too. It's my favorite room in the house – of course!
DEBBIE	¹_____ 's a nice photo. There, on the desk.
ALICIA	Yes, it's me and my family, on vacation in Cancun. We're all very happy in that photo!
DEBBIE	Cool. And is ²_____ your brother?
ALICIA	Yes, it is. ³_____ is Brian.
DEBBIE	Oh, he's nice.
ALICIA	Hmm … sometimes he is, sometimes he isn't.
BRIAN	Alicia! Are you in here?
ALICIA	Hi, Brian. Yes, I'm here. And ⁴_____ is my friend Debbie.
BRIAN	Hi, Debbie. Listen, Alicia – are ⁵_____ your things?
ALICIA	What things?
BRIAN	The books and magazines.
ALICIA	Oh, yes, sorry.
BRIAN	And Alicia, the DVDs on your bed – ⁶_____ are my DVDs!
ALICIA	Yes, you're right. Sorry again.
BRIAN	You know what, Debbie? Sometimes my sister isn't my favorite person!

3 **Complete the dialogue with the words in the list.**

this (x~~2~~) | that (x3) | these | those

GRAMMAR

this / that / these / those

1 **Match the sentences with the pictures. Write 1–4 in the boxes. Then circle the correct words to complete the rule.**

A ☐

B 1

C ☐

D ☐

1 This is my sister.

2 That's my brother.

3 These are my pens.

4 Those are my friends.

> **RULE:** The words **this** and **that** are ¹*singular / plural*.
> The words **these** and **those** are ²*singular / plural*.
> We use **this** and **these** to talk about things that are ³*near to / far from* us.
> We use **that** and **those** to talk about things that are ⁴*near to / far from* us.

2 **Look at the pictures in Exercise 1 again. Complete the sentences with *this, that, these,* or *those*.**

0 Picture A: Is ___*this*___ your phone?

1 Picture B: Are _____ your books?

2 Picture C: Are _____ your books?

3 Picture D: Is _____ your phone?

Workbook page 29

Pronunciation

this / that / these / those

Go to page 120. 🔊

VOCABULARY
House and furniture

1 🔊 1.38 **Match the rooms in the picture with the words. Write 1–7. Listen and check.**

bathroom	
bedroom	
garage	1
backyard	
hall	
kitchen	
living room	

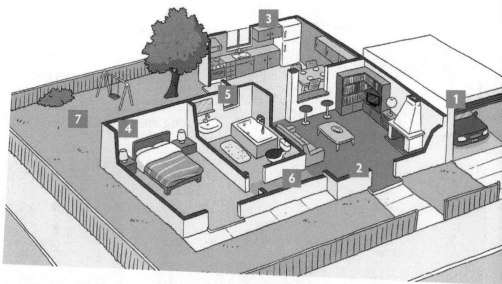

2 🔊 1.39 **Match the words with the photos. Write 1–8 in the boxes. Listen and check.**

1 chair | 2 bathtub | 3 bed | 4 stove | 5 fridge (refrigerator) | 6 shower | 7 couch | 8 toilet

A B C D

E F G 1 H

3 Complete the table with words a–h from Exercise 2.

Living room	Kitchen	Bedroom	Bathroom

4 **SPEAKING** In your notebook, draw an unusual house. Put the furniture in different rooms. Tell your partner about your house.

> The fridge is in the living room.
> The toilet is in the kitchen.

Workbook page 31

WRITING
Your favorite room

1 Think about your favorite room in your house. Answer the questions.

- Which room is it?
- Is it big or small?
- What things are in the room?
- What colors are the things in the room?

2 Write a description of your favorite room (about 50 words).

A song for Ruby

1 **Look at the photos and answer the questions.**

1 Where are the four friends?
2 How does Tom feel in photo 4?

2 🔊 1.40 **Now read and listen to the photostory. What song does Tom's dad want to play?**

TOM Come in, guys.
RUBY Wow, this photo is cool!
TOM Thank you.
DAN What's that photo over there?

1

TOM That's my family. We're on vacation.
RUBY It looks great. So, these are your parents and ...
ELLIE ... that's your sister?
TOM No, that's my cousin. My sister is there.
ELLIE Oh, right. She looks like your sister!

2

DAD Hello, everyone.
DAN Hello.
TOM Dad, these are my friends. This is Dan, and that's Ellie, and this is Ruby.

3

DAD Ruby? Really?
RUBY Yes. Why?
DAD Well, there's a great song called "Ruby." Just a minute. Where's my guitar?
TOM OK, guys, let's go. I want to show you my room.

4

DEVELOPING SPEAKING

3 🎦 EP2 **Watch to find out how the story continues.**

1 What things do Tom's friends like about the house?
2 Do they like Tom's dad?

4 🎦 EP2 **Watch again. Match the parts of the sentences.**

0	Tom isn't very happy	*f*
1	Tom isn't a big fan of auto racing,	
2	The chair in Tom's room	
3	The backyard in Tom's house	
4	Tom's dad's CDs are	
5	Ruby says Tom's dad	

a is broken.
b is really cool.
c in the living room.
d but he likes the poster of a racecar.
e isn't very big.
f about his dad.

PHRASES FOR FLUENCY

1 **Find the expressions 1–4 in the story. Who says them?**

1 Let's go. _____
2 Oh, right. _____
3 Really? _____
4 Just a minute. _____

2 **How do you say the expressions in Exercise 1 in your language?**

3 **Put the sentences in the correct order to make a dialogue.**

1	SALLY	Where are we?
	SALLY	Really? Oh, right. Sorry. Here's the right map.
	SALLY	OK. The map's here. Here you are.
	TOM	Just a minute. Let me look at the map.
	TOM	Thanks. Oh. Sorry, Sally, this is the wrong map.
	TOM	Thanks. Ah, we're on the right road. Let's go.

4 **Complete the mini-dialogues with the expressions from Exercise 1.**

1 A I love this band. They're fantastic.
   B _____ ? I don't like them.
2 A Hey, that's my phone. Your phone is there.
   B _____ . Sorry about that.
3 A Are you ready?
   B _____ , where are my keys?
      Oh, here they are. _____ .

FUNCTIONS
Paying compliments

1 **Read the phrases. Check (✓) four more compliments.**

0	This picture looks cool.	✓
1	Thank you.	
2	That's nice!	
3	That's my family.	
4	That's great.	
5	What a nice (picture)!	
6	I really like (your music).	

2 **Check (✓) the situations when you pay a compliment.**

1 Your friend has a new shirt.
2 It's a sunny day.
3 Your friend's sister is in New York on vacation.
4 There is a great poster on your friend's bedroom wall.
5 It's your friend's birthday.
6 You like your friend's room.

3 **Put the sentences in the correct order to make dialogues.**

1 | 1 | A | This photo is great. |
	A	Is that your sister in the photo? She looks nice.
	B	Yes, her name's Carol. She's 14.
	B	Thanks. I like it, too.

2 | | A | Where's it from? |
	A	I really like your shirt.
	B	Oh, thank you.
	B	It's from my vacation in Brazil.

4 **SPEAKING Act out the dialogues. Then change them and make similar dialogues.**

4 IN THE CITY

READING

1 Match the phrases in the list with the photos. Write 1–4 in the boxes.

1 a famous square | 2 a famous tower
3 a famous palace | 4 a famous statue

2 **SPEAKING** Work in pairs. Can you name the places in the photos? Where are they?

> *I think it's the Eiffel Tower. It's in Paris.*

3 🔊 1.41 Read and listen to the brochure. Which two things in Exercise 1 are in *Window of the World*?

4 Read the brochure again. Mark the sentences T (true) or F (false).

0 *Window of the World* is in China. `T`
1 All the models are of things in the same country.
2 There are models of 130 different things.
3 You can ski at *Window of the World*.
4 There is a train station in the park.
5 There are restaurants at *Window of the World*.

5 **SPEAKING** Work in pairs. Ask and answer the questions.

1 Would you like to go to *Window of the World*?
2 What would you do there?

A

B

C

D `1`

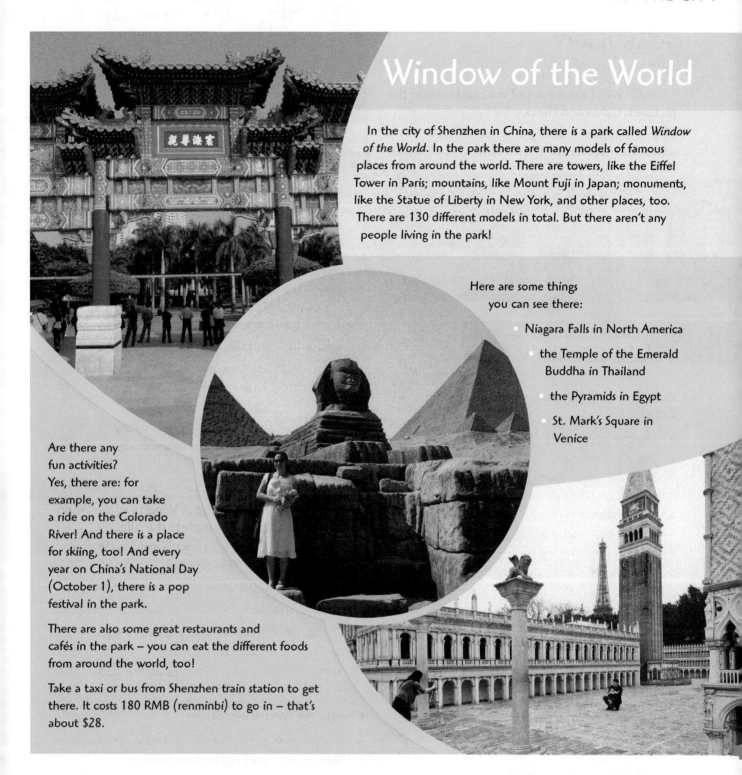

Window of the World

In the city of Shenzhen in China, there is a park called *Window of the World*. In the park there are many models of famous places from around the world. There are towers, like the Eiffel Tower in Paris; mountains, like Mount Fuji in Japan; monuments, like the Statue of Liberty in New York, and other places, too. There are 130 different models in total. But there aren't any people living in the park!

Here are some things you can see there:

- Niagara Falls in North America
- the Temple of the Emerald Buddha in Thailand
- the Pyramids in Egypt
- St. Mark's Square in Venice

Are there any fun activities? Yes, there are: for example, you can take a ride on the Colorado River! And there is a place for skiing, too! And every year on China's National Day (October 1), there is a pop festival in the park.

There are also some great restaurants and cafés in the park – you can eat the different foods from around the world, too!

Take a taxi or bus from Shenzhen train station to get there. It costs 180 RMB (renminbi) to go in – that's about $28.

THiNK VALUES

My town/city

1 **Think of your town/city and answer the questions.**

   1 What are the most interesting places for you?
   2 What are the most interesting places for a visitor?

2 **SPEAKING Make one list of interesting places for you and one for a visitor. Tell a partner.**

   The most interesting places for me in my town/city are …

   The most interesting places in my town/city for a visitor are …

3 **Think of a place/thing in your town, city, or country to put in *Window of the World*.**

   1 What is the name of the place/thing?
   2 Why do you want it in *Window of the World*?

   I want to put … from my city because it's very old and beautiful.

4 **SPEAKING Compare your ideas with others in the class.**

VOCABULARY
Places in a town/city

1 🔊 1.42 **Write the names of the places under the pictures. Listen and check.**

bank | drugstore | library | museum | ~~park~~
post office | restaurant | supermarket | train station

0 _park_
1 _____
2 _____
3 _____
4 _____
5 _____
6 _____
7 _____
8 _____

2 **Complete each sentence with a place from Exercise 1.**

0 You buy milk in a _supermarket_ .
1 You play soccer in a _____ .
2 You eat lunch or dinner in a
   _____ .
3 You send letters in a _____ .
4 You get on a train in a _____ .
5 You buy medicine in a _____ .
6 You look at old and interesting things in a
   _____ .
7 You read books in a _____ .

Workbook page 39 ▶

GRAMMAR

there is / there are

1 **Complete the sentences from the brochure on page 39. Use *is*, *are*, and *aren't*. Then complete the table.**

1 In the city of Shenzhen in China, there
   _____ a park called *Window of the World*.
2 _____ there any fun activities?
3 But there _____ any people living in the park!

	Singular nouns	Plural nouns
Affirmative	There 1_____	There 3_____
Negative	There isn't	There 4_____
Questions	2_____ there?	5_____ there?

2 **Complete the sentences in the positive (+), negative (-), or question (?) form. Use *there is*, *there are*, *is there*, *there aren't*, and *are there*.**

0 _There are_ six bridges in the city.
1 _____ any good movies on TV tonight.
2 _____ a museum in your town?
3 _____ a great café near here.
4 _____ any people in the park today.
5 _____ any nice stores on this street?

some / any

3 **Complete the sentences about *Window of the World* with *some* or *any*. Then complete the rule.**

1 But there aren't _____ people living in the park.
2 Are there _____ fun activities?
3 There are _____ great restaurants and cafés.

> **RULE:** We often use **some** and **any** with plural nouns.
> We use [1]_____ in affirmative sentences.
> We use [2]_____ in negative sentences and questions.

4 **Choose the correct words.**

0 There are (some)/ any interesting things in the museum.
1 There aren't *some* / *any* parks in my town.
2 Are there *some* / *any* good stores here?
3 There are *some* / *any* nice places to eat here.

5 **SPEAKING** **Work in pairs. Think of a city, but don't say the name! Ask and answer questions to find out the cities.**

Is there a famous park in your city?   *Yes, there is.*

Is there a famous statue?   *Yes, there is.*

Is it New York?

Workbook page 36 ▶

VOCABULARY
Prepositions of place

Look at the map and complete the sentences with the words in the list.

behind | between | in front of | next to
~~on the corner (of)~~ | across from

0 A is _on the corner (of)_ Green Street and High Street and _____ the supermarket.

1 B is _____ the library.

2 C is _____ the bank.

3 D is _____ the park and the post office.

4 E is _____ the restaurant.

Workbook page 39

LISTENING

1 🔊 1.43 **Listen to three people asking for directions. Write** *museum, drugstore,* **and** *mall* **in the correct places on the map. There are two extra spaces.**

2 🔊 1.43 **Listen again and complete the sentences.**

  0 The drugstore is _across from_ the library.

  1 The drugstore is _____ the bank.

  2 The museum is on _____ Green Street.

  3 The mall is _____ a restaurant.

GRAMMAR
Imperatives

1 **Complete the examples with** *don't, turn,* **and** *go.* **Then complete the rule.**

  1 _____ past the supermarket.

  2 _____ left.

  3 _____ take a bus – it's only two minutes from here.

> **RULE:** To tell someone to do something, you can use the **imperative** – it's the same as the base form of the verb.
>
> To tell someone **not** to do something, use _____ + the base form of the verb.

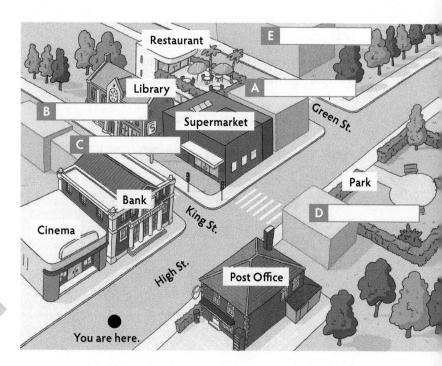

2 **Match the parts of the sentences.**

  0 Listen   b

  1 Sit

  2 Don't open

  3 Don't look

  4 Turn

  5 Go

  a the door.

  b to me.

  c right.

  d down, please.

  e down the street.

  f at the answers.

Workbook page 37

FUNCTIONS
Giving directions

1 SPEAKING **Work in pairs. Look at the map again. Student A: You're at the restaurant. Student B: Think of another place on the map, but don't say it! Tell Student A how to find you.**

> *OK, turn right and right again onto High Street. Turn right on King Street. I'm on the right.*

> *The supermarket?*

> *That's right!*

2 SPEAKING **Now change. Student B: You're in the park. Student A: Choose another place on the map and tell Student B how to get there.**

READING

1 🔊 1.44 **Read and listen to the dialogues. Where are the people? Write a letter in each box. There are two extra letters.**

A bookstore | B drugstore | C shoe store
D supermarket | E train station

1 ☐

MAN	Good morning. Can I ⁰ _help you_ ?
GIRL	Yes, please. A ticket to Chicago, please.
MAN	Round trip?
GIRL	Yes, please. ¹_____ is that?
MAN	Well, it's $27.50, but you can't come back between four and seven o'clock. That costs extra.
GIRL	Oh, no problem. Here you are, $30.
MAN	Thank you. And $2.50 is your change.
GIRL	Thanks a lot. Is that the train?
MAN	Yes, hurry! Oh – don't forget your tickets!
GIRL	Oh, yes – thanks!

2 ☐

WOMAN	These are nice. I really like them.
MAN	Yes, they're really nice.
WOMAN	And they're very comfortable. How much ²_____ ?
MAN	They're $120.
WOMAN	Wow. They're expensive.
MAN	Yes, but they're beautiful shoes.
WOMAN	You're right. OK, I'll ³_____ them.
MAN	Great!

3 ☐

WOMAN	Hello.
GIRL	Hi. ⁴_____ take these, please?
WOMAN	OK. Wow, that's a lot of books.
GIRL	I know! There are twelve. Well, I'm a student.
WOMAN	Oh, I see. That's $135, please.
GIRL	OK. Here's my credit card.
WOMAN	Thank you. And here are your books.
GIRL	Thanks very much.
WOMAN	OK, bye. Have ⁵_____ .
GIRL	You, too.

2 🔊 1.44 **Listen again. Complete the dialogues with the words and phrases in the list.**

a nice day | are they | Can I
~~help you~~ | How much | take

3 **SPEAKING** **Work in pairs. Act out the dialogues.**

VOCABULARY
Numbers 100+

1 🔊 1.45 **Match the words with the numbers. Then listen, check, and repeat.**

0	130	d	4	560	
1	150		5	1,000	
2	175		6	1,200	
3	200		7	2,000	

a five hundred and sixty
b one thousand two hundred
c two hundred
d one hundred and thirty
e one hundred and seventy-five
f one thousand
g two thousand
h one hundred and fifty

> **LOOK!** When a number is more than 100, we can use the word *and*:
>
> *one hundred and twenty* OR *one hundred twenty*
> *two hundred and twelve* OR *two hundred twelve*
>
> We **don't** use the word *and* for numbers 20–99.
>
> *twenty-five* **NOT** ~~twenty and five~~
> *seventy-three* **NOT** ~~seventy and three~~

2 🔊 1.46 **Listen and write the numbers two ways.**

0	_180_	_one hundred and eighty_
1	_____	_____
2	_____	_____
3	_____	_____
4	_____	_____
5	_____	_____

Workbook page 39 ➤

> **Pronunciation**
> **Word stress in numbers**
> **Go to page 120.** 🔊

VOCABULARY
Prices

1 🔊 1.49 **Say these prices. Listen and check.**

  1 $15.00
  2 £25.00
  3 €230.00
  4 $9.99
  5 $21.95
  6 €72.50

2 🔊 1.50 **Listen and look at the prices. Number them in the order you hear them.**

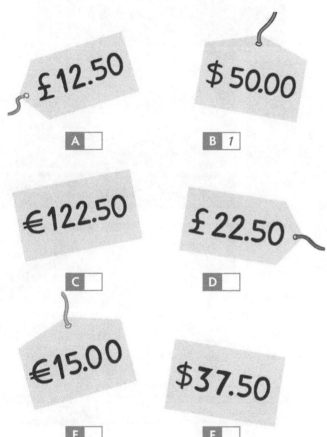

£12.50   A ☐

$ 50.00   B 1

€122.50   C ☐

£22.50   D ☐

€15.00   E ☐

$37.50   F ☐

> **LOOK!** $ = dollar(s)   £ = pound(s)   € = euro(s)
> $2.50 – We say *two dollars and fifty cents* **not** *two dollars fifty*. We can also say *two fifty*.

3 **SPEAKING** Work in pairs. Ask and answer the questions. Student A: Go to page 127. Student B: Go to page 128.

Workbook page 39 →

FUNCTIONS
Buying things in a store

1 **Read these questions and answers. Who says them? Write C (customer) or S (store clerk).**

  1 Can I help you?   S
  2 I'll take them.   ☐
  3 How much are they?   ☐
  4 Here's your change.   ☐
  5 That's $ … , please.   ☐
  6 Do you have …?   ☐

2 **Use the questions and answers from Exercise 1 to complete the dialogue. Write 1–6.**

  A Hi there. __1__
  B Hello. Yes, please. _____ any music magazines?
  A Sure. There's this one here, and there's also this one.
  B Great. _____
  A This one's $3.95, and the other one is $3.50.
  B OK – _____
  A Great. _____ $7.45, _____
  B OK. Here you are. $10.00.
  A Thank you. And _____ – $2.55.
  B Thanks. Bye!

3 🔊 1.51 **Listen and check. Then act out the dialogue with a partner.**

■ TRAIN TO THiNK ■
Exploring numbers

1 **Read, think, and write the answers.**

> Vero, Carlos, and Miguel go shopping. Vero has $20. Carlos has $12, and Miguel has $2. Vero spends $1.40 at the bookstore, $3.30 at the supermarket, and $8.30 at the café. Carlos spends $3.80 at the post office and $2.20 at the drugstore.

At home, Mom says, "How much money do you have now?"
Vero: $_____
Carlos: $_____
Miguel: $_____

2 **Then Mom says: "OK, Carlos and Vero. Give Miguel some money so that you all have the same!"**
Vero gives Miguel $_____ .
Carlos gives Miguel $_____ .

Culture

Parks

around the world

A ☐ Grant Park, Chicago, U.S.A.

There are many parks in Chicago. Grant Park is a very big one. Many tourists and Chicagoans go there every day. There are paths for people on bicycles and there are often music concerts in the park.

B ☐ Stanley Park, Vancouver, Canada

Vancouver is a city near the ocean and mountains. And beautiful Stanley Park is in the city center. More than eight million people go there every year. There are First Nations totem poles in the park.

C ☐ Park Güell, Barcelona, Spain

In this park, designed by Antoni Gaudí, there are houses in many different colors. There are also things like a colorful dragon. From the park you can see the city of Barcelona and the Mediterranean Sea.

D ☐ Ueno Park, Tokyo, Japan

Ueno Park in Tokyo is an old park with hundreds of beautiful cherry trees. In April and May every year, the trees turn pink or white with flowers!

E ☐ The Iguana Park, Guayaquil, Ecuador

The real name of this small park is *Parque Simon Bolivar*, but everyone calls it The Iguana Park because it is full of iguanas. The iguanas are very friendly. People in the city go there and feed them.

F 1 Chapultepec Park, Mexico City, Mexico

This is one of the biggest parks in the Americas. It's a very important green space in this big city. It has a lake and many museums. People in Mexico City love going there – and on Sunday, everything is free!

1 Look at the photos on page 44. Where can you see these things?

a dragon | a lake | cherry trees | mountains
ocean | feed

2 🔊 1.52 Read and listen to the article. Match the photos with the descriptions. Write 1–6 in the boxes.

3 Read the article again. Which parks are these sentences about? Write A–F in the boxes.

0 It isn't a new park.   D
1 There are museums inside the park.
2 You can ride your bicycle in the park.
3 It's possible to see the ocean from the park.
4 People like to feed animals in this park.
5 There are many colorful things in this park.

WRITING
A brochure for your town

1 Read Phil's brochure for his town, Woodstock, New York, U.S.A. What four things does the town have for visitors?

2 Underline the adjectives that Phil uses to describe the good things in the town.

3 Write a brochure for your town/city. Remember to:

- write a sentence to introduce your town (name, where it is)
- say what there is in the town
- give some ideas for things to do there
- write a closing sentence

4 Now write your brochure (35–50 words).

Come to Woodstock!

It's a small, pretty town not far from New York City (two hours away by bus).

- Have something to eat – there are some great restaurants!
- See fantastic views of the countryside.
- Look at art made by local artists in the museum downtown!

Woodstock is famous for music. You can listen to wonderful musicians in cafes, concert halls, and on the streets!

Woodstock – there's something here for everyone!

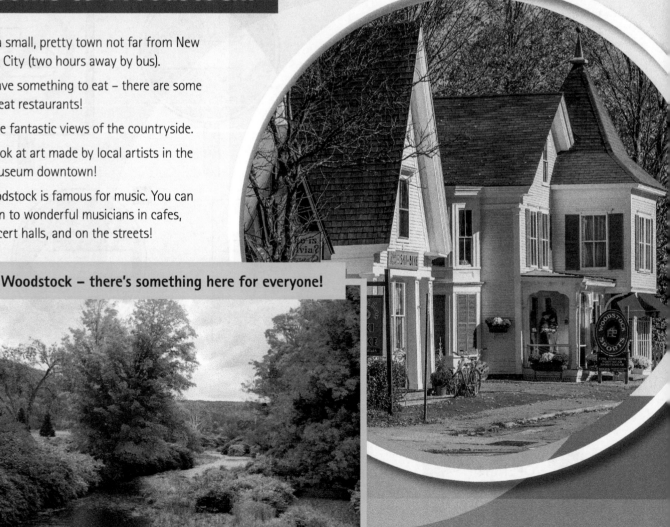

READING AND WRITING
Part 6: Word completion

1 Read the descriptions of some places in a town. What is the word for each one?
The first letter is already there. There is one space for each other letter in the word.

    0 You catch a train here. **s** _t a t i o n_

    1 There are lots of interesting things to see in here. **m** _ _ _ _ _ _

    2 You put your money here. **b** _ _ _ _

    3 Children play here. **p** _ _ _ _

    4 You buy your food here. **s** _ _ _ _ _ _ _ _ _ _ _ _

    5 You sit and eat here. **r** _ _ _ _ _ _ _ _ _ _

Part 1: Matching

2 Which notice (A–H) says this (1–5)? Write the letter A–H in the boxes.

    0 Don't come in here.   G

    1 You can send letters here.

    2 Don't sit here.

    3 Turn left.

    4 The store is not open at 7:30 p.m.

    5 Don't eat here.

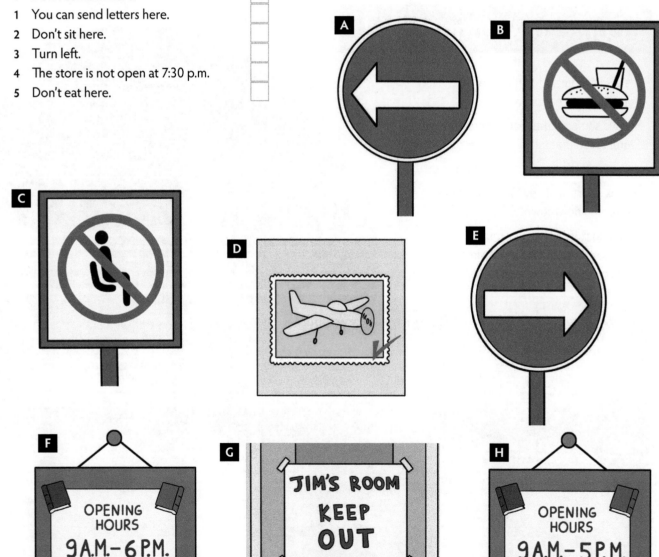

VOCABULARY

1 Complete the sentences with the words in the list. There are two extra words.

backyard | bathroom | stove | garage | grandfather | husband
kitchen | library | on the corner of | across from | couch | wife

1 Come and sit on the _____ . Let's watch TV.
2 There's a new fridge in the _____ . It's really big!
3 There's a _____ next to the fridge in the kitchen.
4 The movie theater is _____ George Street and Smith Street.
5 There's a bathtub and a shower in our _____ .
6 She's Mr. Graham's _____ . Her name's Petra.
7 Our house is nice, but there's no _____ for our car.
8 I need to go to the _____ downtown to get a book for school.
9 The supermarket is _____ the bank.
10 We really love our _____ . He's 72 years old now.

/10

GRAMMAR

2 Complete the sentences with the words in the list.

any | my | some | that | there | those

1 Is _____ a library here?
2 Hey! Is _____ your phone? Don't leave it on the desk.
3 How much are _____ black shoes, please?
4 There aren't _____ good movies on TV tonight.
5 Are you hungry? Eat _____ fruit.
6 Please give me back _____ tablet.

3 Find and correct the mistake in each sentence.

1 There are a really big supermarket in town. _____
2 Do you like me new phone? _____
3 I don't like this shoes. _____
4 Doesn't open the window – it's cold in here! _____
5 That's bike's Jack. _____
6 Come and play at us house. _____

/12

FUNCTIONAL LANGUAGE

4 Complete the missing words.

1 A Hello. Can I h _ _ _ you?
   B Yes, please. H _ _ m _ _ _ are these shoes?
   A $32.99.
   B Great! I'll t _ _ _ them.
2 A Excuse me. W _ _ _ _ is the bank?
   B It's on Green Street. It's n _ _ _ to the supermarket.
   A On Green Street?
   B Yes, walk up here and t _ _ _ left. It's a _ _ _ _ _ from a restaurant.

/8

MY SCORE [   ] /30

| 22 – 30 |
| 10 – 21 |
| 0 – 9 |

47

5 IN MY FREE TIME

OBJECTIVES

FUNCTIONS: talking about habits and activities; talking about technology habits; encouraging someone

GRAMMAR: simple present; adverbs of frequency; simple present (negative and questions)

VOCABULARY: free-time activities; gadgets

A

B 1

C

D

READING

1 Match the activities in the list with the photos. Write 1–4 in the boxes.

1 listen to music | 2 play sports
3 sing | 4 watch TV

2 Read the newsletter quickly. Which of the activities in Exercise 1 does it talk about?

3 🔊 1.53 Read and listen to the newsletter. Mark the sentences T (true) or F (false).

0 Mrs. Hernandez is a math teacher. `T`

1 Glee Club always sings new songs.

2 Glee Club has two concerts every year.

3 Other students always like Glee Club concerts.

4 Glee Club is only for grade seven students.

5 Glee Club meets two times a week.

HOME | ABOUT | NEWS | CONTACT

I love Glee Club!

Our school has a glee club and it's fantastic! I know this because I'm a member. So what is Glee Club? Simple – it's a club for singing, and I love singing.

Mrs. Hernandez is the club leader. She chooses the songs and helps us to learn them. She plays the piano, too. She's really cool and she's really nice. She never gets angry with us. She isn't even the school music teacher. She teaches math. But she just loves singing.

We often sing popular songs from movies, but we sometimes sing old songs from the 1960s and 70s. Three times a year we perform our songs in front of the rest of the school in a special concert. I feel so happy when I'm on stage. The teachers and the other students always cheer when we finish. It feels wonderful.

I love Glee Club. Music is a great way to bring people together. You make so many friends at Glee Club, and not just with the people from your grade. Glee Club is for all ages.

We meet in the auditorium every Tuesday at lunchtime and every Friday after school. Come and join us – we are always happy to see new people!

THiNK VALUES

Better together or better alone?

1 It's good to do some things on your own. But some things are better with a friend. Look at the table and check (✓) the answers for you.

	On my own	With friends
music		
sports		
computer games		
TV		
homework		

2 SPEAKING Tell your partner.

> I listen to music on my own.

GRAMMAR
Simple present

1 **Look at the newsletter on page 49. Complete the sentences with the correct form of the verbs in the list. Then complete the rule.**

cheer | ~~love~~ | make | meet | play

0 I __*love*__ Glee Club!
1 You _____ so many friends at Glee Club.
2 She _____ the piano, too.
3 We _____ in the auditorium.
4 The teachers and the other students always _____ when we finish.

> **RULE:** We add *-s* to the base form of the verb when the subject is *he*, [1]_____, or [2]_____.
>
> **Spelling:** If the verb ends in *consonant + -y*, we change the *y* to an *i* and add *-es*.
> E.g. *study → studies*
> If the verb ends in *-ch*, *-sh*, *-ss*, or *-x*, we add *-es*.
> E.g. *watch → watches*

2 **Write the simple present form of the verbs for *he*, *she*, and *it*.**

0	carry	*carries*
1	choose	_____
2	finish	_____
3	fly	_____
4	get	_____
5	go	_____
6	help	_____
7	love	_____
8	miss	_____
9	study	_____
10	teach	_____
11	watch	_____

> **Pronunciation**
> Simple present verbs: third person
> **Go to page 120.**

Adverbs of frequency

3 **Look at the newsletter on page 49 and complete the sentences. Then complete the rule.**

0 She __*never*__ gets angry with us.
1 We _____ sing popular songs.
2 We _____ sing old songs.
3 We are _____ happy to see new people!

> **RULE:**
> 1 _____ 2 _____ 3 _____ *always*
> 0% ⟶ 100%
> With the verb *be*, the adverb of frequency usually comes [4]*before / after* the verb.
> With other verbs, the adverb of frequency usually comes [5]*before / after* the verb.

Workbook page 46

VOCABULARY
Free-time activities

1 🔊 1.56 **Match the activities in the list with the photos. Write 1–6 in the boxes. Listen and check.**

1 ~~chat with friends online~~ | 2 dance
3 do homework | 4 go shopping
5 hang out with friends | 6 play computer games

A B C D E F *1*

2 **Put the words in order to make sentences.**

0 computer games / in the morning / I / play / never
I never play computer games in the morning.
1 often / with friends / hang out / in the park / We
2 sad / I / when / I'm / never / dance
3 goes / with her mom / She / sometimes / shopping
4 after school / always / his homework / does / He

3 **Complete the sentences with an adverb of frequency so that they are true for you.**

1 I _____ play computer games in the evening.
2 I _____ go shopping with my friends.
3 I _____ do my homework in the morning.
4 I _____ dance in my living room.

4 **SPEAKING Work in pairs. Compare your sentences. Compare with others in the class.**

Workbook page 49

LISTENING

1 🔊1.57 **Listen and write the names under the photos.**

Chris | Kayla | Julia | ~~Tim~~

A _____   B _____

_____   _____
Tim

C _____   D _____

_____   _____

2 🔊1.57 **Listen again and correct the adverb of frequency in each sentence.**

1 Tim sometimes uses the tablet for his homework.
2 Kayla and her brother always watch TV together.
3 Julia never plays *Minecraft™* online with her friends.
4 Chris never uses his phone to text his friends.

3 **SPEAKING** Work in pairs. Tell your partner how you use technology. Use adverbs of frequency.

> *I sometimes use my computer to shop online.*

GRAMMAR
Simple present (negative)

1 **Match the parts of the sentences. Then complete the rule.**

0	I use it to text my friends because	d
1	We never watch TV together in our house,	
2	It's free;	
3	When Mom calls me for dinner,	

a it doesn't cost anything.
b but we use it to play games.
c I don't want to stop playing.
d I don't really like to talk on the phone.

RULE: *Before / After* the verb, we use *don't* and *doesn't* to make negative sentences..

I/you/we/they + ²_____ + base form

he/she/it + ³_____ + base form

NOT *don't/doesn't* + base form + -s, e.g. ~~He doesn't likes music.~~

2 **Make the sentences negative.**

0 I like math.
  I don't like math.

1 The class finishes at two o'clock.
  _____

2 My brother helps me with my homework.
  _____

3 We go swimming on Sundays.
  _____

4 They watch a lot of TV.
  _____

5 My aunt lives in Quito.
  _____

3 **Complete the sentences with the verbs.**

1 I sometimes ___play___ (play) tennis with my mom, but I _____ (not play) it with my dad.
2 My brother _____ (not do) his homework after school. He _____ (do) it in the morning before school.
3 Susie _____ (not hang out) with us after school. She _____ (go) home.
4 I always _____ (listen) to music in the kitchen, but my dad _____ (not like) it.

Workbook page 47 ➔

▇ THiNK SELF-ESTEEM ▇▇▇
What makes you happy?

1 **Check (✓) what makes you happy.**

	Me	My partner
watch TV		
listen to music		
play computer games		
go shopping		
chat with friends online		
hang out with friends		

2 **SPEAKING** Work in pairs. Tell each other about two things that make you feel happy and two things that don't. Then tell the class.

> *I'm happy when I watch TV.*

> *Paolo isn't happy when he goes shopping.*

Does TV control your life?

1 How many hours of TV do you watch every day?

a less than 1   **b** between 1 and 3   **c** more than 3

2 Do you watch TV before school?

a never   **b** sometimes   **c** always

3 Do you watch TV in bed?

a never   **b** sometimes   **c** always

4 Do you watch TV at meal times?

a never   **b** sometimes   **c** always

5 Does your family say that you watch too much TV?

a never   **b** sometimes   **c** always

READING

1 Read the quiz from a teen magazine and choose your answers.

2 SPEAKING Work in pairs. Ask and answer the questions with your partner.

3 Work out your score and read the comment. Do you agree with it?

a = 1 point	**b** = 2 points	**c** = 3 points

5 to 9	No, it doesn't. TV doesn't control your life. You control your TV!
10 to 12	TV doesn't control your life, but watch out!
13 to 15	Yes, it does! TV controls your life! Turn it off and do something different!

GRAMMAR
Simple present (questions)

1 Look back at the quiz. Put the words in order to make questions. Then complete the rule.

1 your / TV / life / control / Does / ?

_____

2 watch / in / you / TV / bed / Do / ?

_____

> **RULE:** To make questions, we use **do** and **does**
> [1]before / after the subject.
> [2]_____ + I/you/we/they + base form
> [3]_____ + he/she/it + base form
>
> To answer questions, we use short answers.
> Yes, I/you/we/they **do**.   No, I/you/we/they **don't**.
> Yes, he/she/it **does**.   No, he/she/it **doesn't**.

2 Choose the correct words.

0 *Do /* (*Does*) *your dad cook?*
1 *Do / Does* your best friend play baseball?
2 *Do / Does* you like pizza?
3 *Do / Does* your parents play computer games?
4 *Do / Does* you usually have a lot of homework?
5 *Do / Does* you hang out with friends after school?

3 Write questions in your notebook.

0 watch TV with your family / you
   Do you watch TV with your family?
1 play tennis / best friend
2 ask for help with housework / your mom and dad
3 like dogs / you
4 take you shopping / your mom
5 listen to music / every day / your friends

4 SPEAKING Work in pairs. Ask and answer the questions in Exercises 2 and 3.

Does your dad cook?

Yes, he does. He sometimes cooks on the weekend.

No, he doesn't. He never cooks.

Workbook page 47

VOCABULARY
Gadgets

1 🔊 1.58 **Match the objects in the list with the pictures. Write 1–8 in the boxes. Listen and check.**

1 e-reader | 2 game console | 3 GPS
4 headphones | 5 laptop | 6 MP3 player
7 smartphone | 8 tablet

A ▢

B ▢

C ▢

D ▢

E ☐ 1

F ▢

2 SPEAKING **Look at the table and make sentences.**

I use / don't use my	tablet game console MP3 player smartphone GPS laptop e-reader headphones	to	play computer games. shop. listen to music. do homework. read books/magazines. talk to my friends. watch TV. find out which way to go.

G ▢

3 SPEAKING **Work in pairs. Tell your partner which of these gadgets you use every day.**

I use a tablet every day.

I don't use a laptop every day.

H ▢

Workbook page 49

WRITING
Days in your life

1 🔊 1.59 **Complete the days of the week with the missing vowels. Listen and check.**

M _o_ nd _a_ y
T _ _ _ sd _ _ y
W _ dn _ sd _ _ y
Th _ _ rsd _ _ y
Fr _ _ d _ _ y
S _ t _ _ rd _ _ y
S _ _ nd _ _ y

2 **What do you do or not do on different days? Choose three days and make notes.**

⦿ Sunday   – baseball
⦿   – no school
⦿

3 **Write about three days of the week.**

I like Sundays because I always play baseball and I don't go to school. It's a great day.

The school play

1 **Look at the photos and answer the questions.**

1 Who can you see in the first photograph?
2 How do Tom and Ellie feel in photo 2?

2 🔊1.60 **Now read and listen to the photostory. What does Ruby agree to do?**

RUBY Where are Tom and Ellie?
DAN They're at Drama Club practice. They're in the school play, remember?
RUBY Oh, that's right. They're amazing.
DAN What do you mean?
RUBY To be in a play in front of the whole school.

1

DAN Look. Here they are. They don't look very happy.
RUBY Hi, guys. What's wrong?
TOM It's Anna Williams. She's in the play, but she's sick.
ELLIE We really need her. The play is on Friday.

2

ELLIE I have an idea. Ruby, do you want to be in the play? You can have Anna's part.
RUBY Me! No way!
TOM Oh, come on, Ruby. Please. We really need you.
DAN Do it, Ruby. Help your friends.

3

Am I crazy?

RUBY Oh, OK.
ELLIE I love you, Ruby! Thank you so much.
TOM Yes, you're the best.
RUBY Am I crazy?

4

DEVELOPING SPEAKING

3 ▶ EP3 **Watch to find out how the story continues.**

Does Ruby do the play?

4 ▶ EP3 **Watch again. Correct the false information in the sentences.**

0 Ruby is excited about the play.
  Ruby is nervous about the play.
1 The performance is four days away.
2 In the play, Ruby wants to speak to the queen.
3 Dan says he has some bad news for Ruby.
4 Ruby is sick.
5 Anna doesn't want to be in the play.

PHRASES FOR FLUENCY

1 **Find the expressions 1–4 in the story. Who says them?**

1 What's wrong?   _____
2 I have an idea.   _____
3 No way!   _____
4 Come on.   _____

2 **How do you say the expressions in Exercise 1 in your language?**

3 **Put the sentences in the correct order to make a dialogue.**

a	☐	MOLLY	Oh, come on, Ben. Please!
b	☐	MOLLY	It's my homework. Can you help me with it?
c	☐	MOLLY	Very funny, Ben.
d	1	MOLLY	Hi, Ben. Listen. I have a problem.
e	☐	BEN	No way! I always help you with homework.
f	☐	BEN	Oh? What's wrong?
g	☐	BEN	No! But listen – I have an idea. Ask Mom!

4 **Complete the dialogues with the expressions from Exercise 1.**

0 A I'm bored.
  B Me, too. _I have an idea._ Let's play ball in the park.
1 A Can I talk to you? I have a problem.
  B Really? _____
2 A I don't want to come to the party.
  B Oh, _____, Jen. Parties are great!
3 A Come to the football game with me.
  B _____ I don't like football.

FUNCTIONS
Encouraging someone

1 **Put the words in order to make sentences.**

I'm worried. I don't want to do it.

1 are / you / great
  _____

2 can / do / it / you
  _____

3 worry / don't
  _____

4 here / I'm / help / you / to
  _____

2 **Choose a picture and write a dialogue.**

3 SPEAKING **Work in pairs. Act out the dialogue.**

6 FRIENDS

READING

1 Match the things in the list with the photos. Write 1–6 in the boxes.

1 a woman with a child | 2 a shaved head
3 short black hair | 4 green eyes
5 a doctor and a nurse | 6 long curly hair

2 SPEAKING Work in pairs. Complete the sentences. Tell your partner.

My eyes are _____ .
My hair is _____ .
My best friend's eyes are _____ .
My mom's hair is _____ .

> My eyes are brown.

3 ◀)) 1.61 Read and listen to the article. What's wrong with Delaney?

4 Read the article again. Match the parts of the sentences.

0 Delaney is 11, and the girls and boys   e

1 The doctors say that she

2 She's in the hospital for months, and this

3 Delaney doesn't have any hair,

4 Kamryn shaves her head and

5 The teachers at the school don't want Kamryn

a has a terrible disease – cancer.
b that makes Delaney really happy.
c and her friend Kamryn wants to help her.
d at school with a shaved head.
e in her class like her a lot.
f is difficult for her, but she's strong.

A

B

C

D
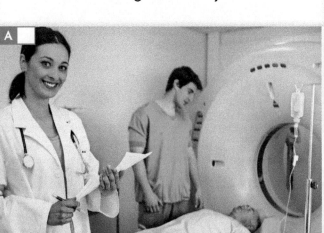

E

F 1

A real friend

Best Friends

Delaney Clements is 11. She has a big smile and beautiful hair. She's a very active girl, and she loves sports. Delaney is very popular with her classmates. Her best friend is a girl named Kamryn. She's in Delaney's class.

One day Delaney is very tired and feels bad. Her mom and dad take her to the hospital. The doctors check the girl. They say that Delaney is very sick. She has cancer. Her parents are very worried.

Delaney is in the hospital for months. It's a very difficult time for her, but she often smiles. The doctors and nurses like her a lot. She's a very strong girl.

Delaney looks very different now. She doesn't have any hair. Delaney feels very different from her classmates. But she has a real friend, Kamryn. Kamryn talks to her parents. She wants to help Delaney. She wants to look like Delaney. Kamryn shaves her head. When Delaney sees her friend without hair, she's very happy. Now both girls don't have any hair. Now Delaney isn't alone. She has a wonderful friend.

But there is a terrible surprise for Kamryn the next day at school. Her teachers say it isn't OK to have a shaved head. They don't want Kamryn to go to school with a shaved head.

A lot of people don't understand the teachers, and they tell the school what they think. The newspapers have lots of stories about the two girls.

In the end, the teachers say it's OK. Kamryn goes back to school.

■ THiNK VALUES

Helping a friend

SPEAKING **How can you help a friend in these situations? Work in pairs. Use the suggestions in the list and your own ideas.**

I help him/her study. | I talk to him/her.
I make him/her a sandwich. | I lend him/her my tablet.
I give him/her a hug.

1   My friend is sad.
2   My friend gets a bad grade on his/her math test.
3   My friend is hungry and doesn't have anything to eat.
4   My friend's computer is broken.
5   My friend has a problem at school.

GRAMMAR
have (affirmative and negative)

1 **Look at the article on page 57. Choose the correct form of *have* in the sentences. Then complete the rule and the table.**

1 She *have / has* a big smile.
2 Now both girls *don't have / doesn't have* any hair.
3 The newspapers *has / have* lots of stories about the two girls.

> **RULE:** We use *have* and *don't have* or *has* and _____ *have* to talk about possession.

Affirmative	Negative
I/You/We/They ¹_____ a problem.	I/You/We/They ²_____ **have** a problem. (**do not have**)
He/She/It ³_____ a problem.	He/She/It **doesn't have** a problem. (**does not have**)

2 **Complete the sentences with the correct form of *have*.**

0 This computer is $700. I ___*don't have*___ the money to buy it.
1 My best friend Tony _____ any sisters, but he _____ two brothers.
2 I _____ a tablet, but I really want one.
3 I _____ a new smartphone. Here's my new number.
4 Jorge and Maria _____ a car, but they have bikes.
5 Lara _____ a big family. She _____ three sisters and four brothers.

Workbook page 54

VOCABULARY
Parts of the body

1 🔊 1.62 **Label the picture with the words in the list. Listen and check.**

arm | body | ear | eye | face | foot | hand | leg
mouth | nose

2 **SPEAKING** **Work in pairs. Look at the picture and labels for 30 seconds. Then cover the labels. Test your partner.**

> *What's number 8?*

> *It's an arm.*

Workbook page 57

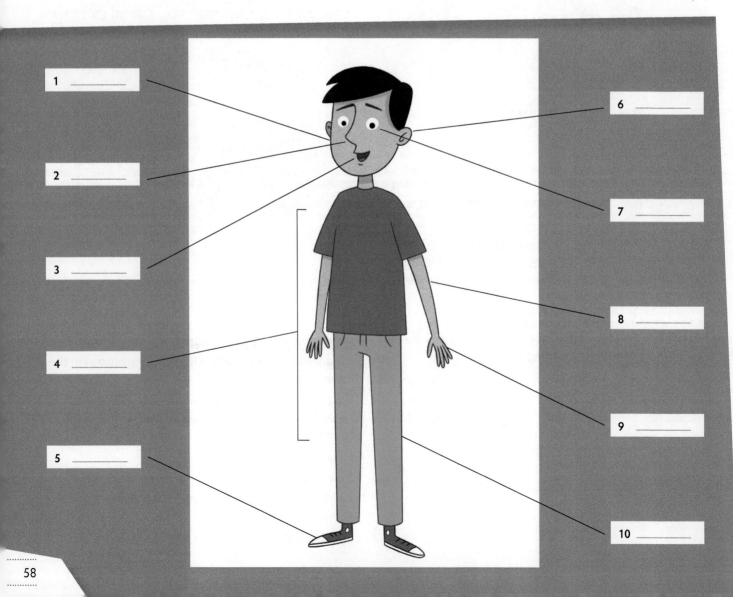

1 _____
2 _____
3 _____
4 _____
5 _____
6 _____
7 _____
8 _____
9 _____
10 _____

LISTENING

1 Which of these sentences do you agree with?

1 It's good to give little gifts to your friends sometimes.
2 A friendship band is a great gift.
3 I really like friendship bands.

2 Read the text. Then answer the question.

Why do people like friendship bands?

_____

3 ◀))1.63 Listen to an interview with 12-year-old Ella Winston. What are her hobbies?

4 ◀))1.63 Listen again and complete the sentences.

0 Ella has five or six _friendship bands_ .
1 She has two or three _____ .
2 In total, she has about _____ friends.
3 She spends about _____ a day making friendship bands.
4 The rubber bands are not _____ .
5 Sometimes, she uses seven or eight different _____ .

Friendship bands

David Beckham has one. The Duchess of Cambridge has one. Harry Styles from One Direction has one. And millions of other young and old people have them, too. Friendship bands are popular all over the world. They are fun and look cool. And, they help us to think of our friends.

GRAMMAR
have (questions)

1 Match the questions and answers. Complete the table.

1 Do you have a hobby? ☐
2 Does your sister have a smartphone? ☐
3 Do your teachers have friendship bands? ☐

a Yes, she does.
b No, they don't.
c Yes, I do.

Questions	Short answers
Do I/you/we/they **have** a hobby?	Yes, I/you/we/they **do**. No, I/you/we/they **don't**. (**do not**)
¹_____ he/she/it **have** a problem?	Yes, she/he/it ²_____ . No, she/he/it ³_____ . (**does not**)

2 Answer the questions.

1 Do you have a TV in your bedroom?
2 Do you have a TV in your kitchen?
3 Do you have a big backyard?
4 Do you have a big family?
5 Does your best friend have a big family?
6 Do you have a lot of songs on your phone?

3 SPEAKING Walk around the classroom. Ask and answer the questions in Exercise 2. Find someone with the same answers as you.

Count and noncount nouns

4 Complete the table with the words in the list and a/an or some. Then complete the rule.

apples | ~~arm~~ | ~~bikes~~ | chairs | color | ~~friend~~
fun | hobby | money | pens | ~~time~~ | work

Count (singular)	Count (plural)	Noncount
an arm a friend	some bikes	some time

RULE: You can count **count** nouns (*two friends, four bikes*).

With singular **count** nouns, we use *a* or ¹_____ .

You can't count **noncount** nouns (*time, water*).

With **noncount** nouns and plural **count** nouns, we use ²_____ .

Workbook page 55 ►

59

READING

1 🔊 1.64 **Read and listen to the dialogue. What's the surprise for Olivia?**

OLIVIA	Hey, Chloe, how are you?
CHLOE	Hi, Olivia. I'm fine, how are you?
OLIVIA	I'm happy. You know my brother, Patrick, right? Well, he has a new friend. He's really cool.
CHLOE	Really? Who is he? What does he look like?
OLIVIA	Well, he has black hair. It's short, and it's curly.
CHLOE	Is he tall or short?
OLIVIA	Pretty tall, and good-looking. He has brown eyes, and he wears glasses.
CHLOE	Brown eyes and glasses?
OLIVIA	Umm … yes, and he has a very nice smile. He's so friendly.
CHLOE	I know.
OLIVIA	You know?
CHLOE	He likes soccer and tennis, and his name's Josh, right?
OLIVIA	That's right, but … but …
CHLOE	And he has a sister?
OLIVIA	How do you know?
CHLOE	Josh is my brother.
OLIVIA	No way!

2 **Which picture shows Josh?**

1	2	3

VOCABULARY
Describing people (1)

1 **Look at the words in the list. Write them under the correct headings. Some words can go under more than one heading.**

~~blue~~ | ~~gray~~ | ~~long~~ | curly | short | black | blond
red | brown | wavy | straight | green

eye color	hair color	hair style
blue	*gray*	*long*

2 **SPEAKING Work in pairs. Use the words in Exercise 1 to describe the people in the photos.**

James Rodriguez   Pink

George Clooney   Shakira

James Rodriguez has …

Pink has …

Workbook page 57

Pronunciation
The /eɪ/ vowel sound
Go to page 120. 🔊

Describing people (2)

3 🔊 1.67 **Match the words in the list with the pictures. Write 1–7 in the boxes. Listen and check.**

1 ~~beard~~ | 2 earrings | 3 glasses
4 mustache | 5 short | 6 smile | 7 tall

A 1
B
C
F
G

D

E

4 🔊 1.68 **Put the words in the correct order to make sentences. Listen and check. Then match each sentence with a picture in Exercise 3.**

0 has / smile / a / she / nice / very   F
   She has a very nice smile.

1 she / glasses / wears   ☐
_____

2 mustache / has / a / he   ☐
_____

3 has / earrings / she / her / ears / in   ☐
_____

4 she / isn't / short; / very tall / she's   ☐
_____

5 🔊 1.69 **Complete the dialogue with the missing words. Listen and check.**

A I have a new friend. His name's Eric.
B What does he look like?
A He has short brown ⁰h *air*_____ , blue ¹e_____ , and he wears ²g_____ .
B Is he tall or ³s_____ ?
A He isn't very tall.
B Is he nice?
A He's very nice and friendly. He has a nice ⁴s_____ .

6 **SPEAKING** **Work in pairs. Act out the dialogue.**

Workbook page 57

FUNCTIONS
Describing people

1 **Complete the dialogue with answers a–d.**

A I'm thinking of a famous basketball player.
B What does he look like?
A ⁰ *d*_____
B What's he like?
A ¹_____
B Is he American?
A ²_____
B Is it LeBron James?
A ³_____

a Yes, he is.
b Yes, it is.
c He's really nice.
d He's tall and strong. He has short brown hair and sometimes a short beard, too. He has a great smile.

2 **SPEAKING** **Work in pairs. Think of a famous person. Ask and answer questions to guess who he/she is.**

I'm thinking of a famous female singer.

What color hair does she have?

▌TRAIN TO THiNK ▌
Attention to detail

1 **SPEAKING** **Work in pairs. Student A: Go to page 127. Student B: Go to page 128. Describe the people in your picture. Find the six differences.**

2 **SPEAKING** **Tell others in the class what differences you find.**

In picture A, the waiter has gray hair. In picture B, ...

Culture

Welcoming people around the world

What do you do when you see someone you know? Do you smile? Do you say hello? Do you touch the other person?

Here are some ideas for travelers. They tell you how people in different countries and cultures welcome each other. Do you do different things in your country?

In many countries in Asia, people bow when they greet each other. This shows respect. In Thailand, people put their hands together and bow. This is called the *wai*.

Western countries

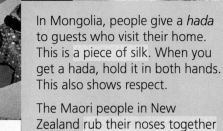

In Mongolia, people give a *hada* to guests who visit their home. This is a piece of silk. When you get a hada, hold it in both hands. This also shows respect.

The Maori people in New Zealand rub their noses together when they meet. This greeting is called the *hongi*.

In Western countries, many people shake hands when they greet each other. Sometimes they just smile and say something like "Hello!" or "Hi!"

In many countries around the world, friends greet by kissing on the cheek. In some countries they kiss on one cheek, in others they kiss both cheeks, and in some they kiss cheeks three times.

1 **Look at the photos and find the actions or objects in the list.**

bow | kiss | a piece of silk
put your hands together | rub noses
shake hands | smile | touch

2 **What do the photos show?**

A people saying hello
B people helping people
C people saying "Thank you."

3 [🔊 1.70] **Read and listen to the article. Write the names of the places under the photos.**

4 **Mark the sentences T (true) or F (false).**

0	The *bow* is a greeting tradition in Asia.	T
1	In Thailand, people rub their noses to say hello.	
2	When you get a *hada*, don't hold it in one hand.	
3	Maori people use the *hongi* to say hello.	
4	In Western countries, people never shake hands.	
5	Only Maori people greet others with a kiss.	
6	In some countries, people kiss three times.	

5 [SPEAKING] **Discuss with a partner.**

1 Which is your favorite way of welcoming people described in the text?
2 How do you welcome other people in your country?

WRITING
Describing a friend

1 **Read the text. Check (✓) the correct picture of James.**

1 ☐

2 ☐

3 ☐

My best friend is named James Webb. He's tall. He has short curly black hair, and he wears glasses. He's in my school, and he always helps me in my classes. After school we always play soccer in the park, and on weekends we often go swimming together. He's a really friendly boy, and he has a very nice smile. He's very popular and everyone likes him. But I'm his best friend!

2 **Read the text again. Complete the notes about James.**

> **Appearance:** hair – _____, _____,
> and _____
> wears _____
> tall
> has a nice smile

> **Personality:** friendly – (nice smile!)
> _____ – (has lots of friends)

3 **Think about your best friend. Make notes.**

> **Appearance:**
> _____
> _____
> _____
> _____

> **Personality:**
> _____
> _____
> _____
> _____

4 **Answer the questions about your best friend.**

1 What's his/her name?
2 How do you know him/her?
3 Why do you like him/her?
4 What do you do together?

5 **Use your notes from Exercises 3 and 4 to write a short description (35–50 words) about your best friend.**

■ THiNK EXAMS ■

READING AND WRITING
Part 4: Multiple-choice reading comprehension

1 Read the article about a school club.

For each sentence, choose the correct answer A, B, or C.

Our school has a LEGO club and it's a lot of fun. It's on Tuesday and Thursday at lunchtime, from 12 p.m. to 1 p.m. I'm a member of the club and so is my best friend, Ally.

Mr. Thomas is the club manager, and the club meets in his classroom, 3T. He has five big boxes of LEGO bricks.

Every week he spends the first 15 minutes showing us different ways to build things. We then practice this for the rest of the time. He sometimes holds contests. The prize is always a small box of LEGOs.

This month there is a contest for all schools in the state to build a LEGO classroom. The prize is a school trip to LEGOLAND. I hope our club wins!

0 The LEGO club is at _____ .
  A the library   B the museum   Ⓒ school

1 The club meets _____ times a week.
  A two   B three   C four

2 The meetings are for _____ .
  A 15 minutes   B 30 minutes   C 60 minutes

3 Mr. Thomas teaches in _____ 3T.
  A school   B classroom   C box

4 Mr. Thomas shows the students how to make things with LEGOs for _____ .
  A 15 minutes   B 30 minutes   C one hour

5 The prize for the LEGO classroom contest is a _____ .
  A LEGO model   B LEGO book   C trip to LEGOLAND

Part 9: Guided writing

2 Read the email from your pen pal Kelly.

From: Kelly
To:

Please tell me about the things you do in your free time. What do you do after school? What do you do on the weekends?

From:
To:

Write an email to Kelly and answer the questions.
Write 25–35 words.

TEST YOURSELF

 UNITS 5 & 6

VOCABULARY

1 Complete the sentences with the words in the list. There are two extra words.

arm | beard | curly | dance | do | earrings | eyes | glasses | go | headphones | out | short

1 No, I can't go out. I need to _____ my homework.
2 I always use _____ when I listen to music at home.
3 She has a friendship band on her left _____ .
4 It's OK music, but you can't _____ to it.
5 My eyes aren't very good. That's why I wear _____ .
6 Let's _____ shopping tomorrow afternoon.
7 He has a big black _____ and mustache.
8 I like her hair. It's long and _____ .
9 Many new babies have blue _____ , but the color changes later.
10 I want to go and hang _____ with my friends this evening.

`/10`

GRAMMAR

2 Put the words in order to make sentences or questions.

1 like / shopping / She / doesn't
2 never / They / to / listen / rock music
3 any / have / on your phone / You / songs / don't
4 She / money / has / some
5 always / I / late / to school / get
6 in English / Do / you / have / books
7 usually / are / tired / on Sunday evenings / We

3 Find and correct the mistake in each sentence.

1 I go often to the movie theater.
2 They listen not to rap music.
3 He play computer games all the time.
4 There is two TVs in my bedroom.
5 She don't do her homework.
6 I have a work to do tonight.
7 We doesn't have any favorite movies.

`/14`

FUNCTIONAL LANGUAGE

4 Write the missing words.

1 A There's a new girl in our class.
  B Oh? What's she _____ ?
  A She's nice. But she _____ talk a lot.
  B Oh. And what does she _____ like?
  A She's tall and she has long black hair.

2 A Are you OK?
  B No. I can't do this homework.
  A Don't _____ . I can help you.
  B Oh, thanks. You _____ great!
  A No problem. I'm here to _____ you.

`/6`

MY SCORE `/30`

| 22 – 30 |
| 10 – 21 |
| 0 – 9 |

65

PRONUNCIATION

UNIT 1
/h/ or /w/ in question words

1 🔊 1.18 **Read and listen to the questions.**

How old are you?
Where are you from?
What's your favorite food?
Who's your favorite soccer player?
Why do you like him?

2 Say the question words in blue.

3 🔊 1.19 **Listen again and repeat. Then practice with a partner.**

UNIT 2
Vowel sounds: adjectives

1 🔊 1.27 **Read and listen to the dialogue.**

TOM   Mom's hungry.
EMILY   Mom? But why? Why is she angry?
TOM   I said Mom's hungry. She wants a sandwich.
EMILY   Oh … OK. Well, Dad's angry.
TOM   Does he want us to make a sandwich for him, too?
EMILY   No! I said he's angry.

2 Which sounds are different in *hungry* and *angry*? Say them and make the differences clear.

3 🔊 1.28 **Listen again and repeat. Then practice with a partner.**

UNIT 3
this / that / these / those

1 🔊 1.36 **Read and listen to the dialogue.**

ANNA   Can I have that cake, please?
CLERK   This one or that one?
ANNA   That one – the chocolate one.
CLERK   That's a carrot cake, but these cupcakes are chocolate.
ANNA   Oh! Can I have two of those?
CLERK   Of course. Here you are.

2 Say the words *that, this, those,* and *these.*

3 🔊 1.37 **Listen again and repeat. Then practice with a partner.**

UNIT 4
Word stress in numbers

1 🔊 1.47 **Read and listen to the dialogue.**

MARCO   It's my sister's birthday today. She's thirteen.
JULIE   Thirty! That's old!
MARCO   Thirty? No! Thirteen.
JULIE   Oh … thirteen. She's the same age as me.

2 Where is the stress on the red words? Where is the stress on the blue words?

3 🔊 1.48 **Listen again and repeat. Then practice with a partner.**

UNIT 5
Simple present verbs: third person

1 🔊 1.54 **Read and listen to the sentences.**

Liz catches the bus to school every morning.
She teaches French at a high school.
At 4:30 she finishes work.
After dinner Liz washes the dishes.
Before she goes to bed, she chooses her clothes for the next day.

2 How many syllables are there in *catch*? How many syllables are there in *catches*? Say the words in blue.

3 🔊 1.55 **Listen again and repeat. Then practice with a partner.**

UNIT 6
The /eɪ/ vowel sound

1 🔊 1.65 **Read and listen to the dialogue.**

REPORTER   I'm sorry I'm late.
WAITER   That's OK. But Jane's waiting for you.
REPORTER   Jane? The girl with long, straight hair?
WAITER   No. Her hair's wavy and gray.
REPORTER   Oh! The woman with the pink face? The one eating cake?
WAITER   Shh! She's famous! She's a great baker!

2 Say the words in blue. Which vowel sound do they all have?

3 🔊 1.66 **Listen again and repeat. Then practice with a partner.**

 GET IT RIGHT!

UNIT 1
The verb *be*

> Learners often leave out *am*, *are*, or *is* in sentences.
>
> We use the subject + *be* + object.
> ✓ *I'm from Chile.*
> ✗ *I from Chile.*
>
> In questions, we use *be* + subject + object + ? .
> ✓ *Are they from Mexico?*
> ✗ *They from Mexico?*

Check (✓) the correct sentences and put an ✗ next to the incorrect ones. Correct the errors.

0 He my favorite sportsperson.   ✗
   He's my favorite sportsperson.
1 The house very big. ☐
2 How old you? ☐
3 I'm from Chicago. ☐
4 You 13 years old? ☐
5 What your name? ☐
6 My favorite singer is Sam Smith. ☐
7 My name John. ☐
8 Houston in Texas? ☐

Subject pronouns and *be*

> Learners sometimes forget the subject pronoun when using *be*.
>
> We always use the subject + *be*.
> ✓ *This is Miguel. He is from Veracruz.*
> ✗ *This is Miguel. Is from Veracruz.*

Correct the sentences.

0 I like Maria. Is very funny.
   I like Maria. She is very funny.
1 I like Florida. Is very hot.
2 It's a taxi. Is yellow.
3 She's my friend. Is from Mexico.
4 They are singers. Are in One Direction.
5 He's my brother. Is 15 years old.
6 I like this phone because is very small.

UNIT 2
be questions

> Learners make mistakes with word order in *be* questions.
>
> In affirmative sentences, we use subject + *be*. In questions, we use the order *be* + subject + (object)+ ? .
> ✓ *That is OK.*
> ✓ *Is that OK?*
> ✗ *That is OK?*

Put the words in the correct order to make questions.

0 it / expensive / is / ?
   Is it expensive?
1 this / is / problem / a / ?
2 on / vacation / are / you / ?
3 how / you / are / ?
4 a / is / famous person / he / ?
5 video game / this / is / your / ?
6 she / is / sister / your / ?

Spelling

> Learners sometimes have problems spelling words in English.
> ✓ *That is my pencil.*
> ✗ *That is my pensil.*

Correct the spelling mistake in the sentences.

0 She is my frind.
   She is my friend.
1 My brother is very funy.
2 The food is excelent.
3 My shirt is withe.
4 We play baseball in the evining.
5 I saw her yesterday moring.
6 The movie is greate.

UNIT 3
Possessive 's

> Learners find it difficult to use possessive 's. They often avoid using it.
>
> We use person + possessive 's + thing/person.
>
> ✓ This is my brother's car.
> ✗ This is ~~the car of my brother~~.

Rewrite the sentences using possessive 's.

0   I went to the house of my cousin.
  I went to my cousin's house.
1   It is the homework of my sister.
2   The name of my friend is Emily.
3   I was at the party of my friend.
4   The family of my friend lives in South Korea.
5   It is the birthday of my sister.
6   This is the bedroom of my brother.

Family vocabulary

> Learners sometimes make spelling mistakes with family words.
>
> ✓ This is my cousin Elena.
> ✗ This is my ~~cousine~~ Elena.
> ✗ This is my ~~couzin~~ Elena.

Correct the spelling mistakes in the family words.

0   How is your familly?
  How is your family?
1   My mather is in the hospital.
2   We go to my granmother's house.
3   I watch movies with my borther.
4   It was a gift from my fater.
5   He is the president's sun.
6   He has two daugthers.

UNIT 4
There is / there are

> Learners sometimes leave out *there* when *there is/are* is required.
>
> We use *there* + *be* + noun, when *be* agrees with the noun. We do not use *there have* or *there has*.
>
> ✓ There is a great café on this street.
> ✗ ~~Is a great café~~ on this street.
> ✗ ~~There has a great café~~ on this street.

Correct the mistakes in the sentences.

0   Next week is a party.
  Next week there is a party.
1   In the kitchen are two windows.
2   In Manhattan there has a nice park.
3   Are any other drinks?
4   In my room there has a bed.
5   It is great because are lots of stores.
6   Near my city there have many interesting places.

Prepositions of place

> Learners sometimes make mistakes with the form of prepositions of place, either misspelling them or using the wrong words.
>
> ✓ The bookstore is next to the post office.
> ✗ The bookstore is ~~next the post office~~.

Correct the mistakes in the sentences.

0   My house is acros from the school.
  My house is across from the school.
1   The restaurant is infront of the bank.
2   My house is nex to Park Hotel.
3   I live behing the station.
4   Station Road is beetween the supermarket and the post office.
5   The drugstore is across to the museum.
6   Their houses are next the hospital.

UNIT 5
Simple present: affirmative

> **Learners often make agreement mistakes in the simple present.**
>
> ✓ *It helps me with my studies.*
> ✗ *It ~~help~~ me with my studies.*

Correct the mistakes in the sentences.

0   He play soccer.
   He plays soccer.
1   Every day he eat breakfast.
2   They likes sports.
3   She go to college.
4   Angela work Monday to Friday.
5   People plays games on their phones.
6   School start on Friday.

Simple present: negative

> **Learners sometimes make agreement mistakes in the simple present negative.**
>
> **The verb *do* agrees with the person and number of the subject.**
>
> ✓ *He doesn't like sports.*
> ✗ *He ~~don't~~ like sports.*

Choose the correct words in the sentences.

0   They (don't)/ doesn't understand.
1   She *doesn't / don't* have any time.
2   He *doesn't / don't* like candy.
3   We *doesn't / don't* need to wear sports clothes.
4   It *don't / doesn't* cost much.
5   My teacher *don't / doesn't* give me a lot of homework.
6   I *don't / doesn't* like video games.

UNIT 6
Count and noncount nouns

> **Learners sometimes confuse *a/an* with *some*.**
>
> **We use *a/an* with count nouns in the singular. We use *some* for count nouns in the plural.**
>
> ✓ *We can buy a gift for his birthday.*
> ✗ *We can buy ~~some gift~~ for his birthday.*
> ✓ *We can buy some gifts for his birthday.*
>
> **We also use *some* with noncount nouns.**
>
> ✓ *You need some water.*
> ✗ *You need ~~a water~~.*

Choose the correct words in the sentences.

0   I have *some /*(a)T-shirt.
1   We took a break and ate *some / a* sandwich.
2   The best gift was *some / a* jacket.
3   I have *some / a* good news.
4   Can you take *some / a* photo of us?
5   I listen to *some / a* music with my family.
6   He has *some / a* good friends.

This page is intentionally left blank.

STUDENT A

UNIT 4, PAGE 43, VOCABULARY

UNIT 6, PAGE 61, TRAIN TO THINK

Student A

Ask and answer the questions with your partner.

£400.00

$90.00

€4.25

$7.50

How much is the TV?

It's …

How much are the …?

They're …

Student A

Describe to your partner what the people in your picture look like. Your partner describes what the people in his/her picture look like. Find the six differences.

STUDENT B

UNIT 4, PAGE 43, VOCABULARY

UNIT 6, PAGE 61, TRAIN TO THINK

Student B

Ask and answer the questions with your partner.

$200.00

$15.00

$8.50

€3.80

How much is the TV?

It's ...

How much are the ...?

They're ...

Student B

Describe to your partner what the people in your picture look like. Your partner describes what the people in his/her picture look like. Find the six differences.

Acknowledgments

The authors and publishers acknowledge the following sources of copyright material and are grateful for the permissions granted. While every effort has been made, it has not always been possible to identify the sources of all the material used, or to trace all copyright holders. If any omissions are brought to our notice, we will be happy to include the appropriate acknowledgments on reprinting.

The publishers are grateful to the following for permission to reproduce copyright photographs and material:

T = Top, B = Below, L = Left, R = Right, C = Center, B/G = Background

p.5 (TL): © Zoonar GmbH / Alamy; p.5 (TC): Foodcollection / Getty Images; p.5 (TR): Peshkova / Getty Images; p.5 (TL): fStop Images / Getty Images; p.5 (TC): © Ivan Vdovin / Alamy; p.5 (TR): © Michael Dwyer / Alamy; p.5 (CL): vsl / Shutterstock; p.5 (CL): © YAY Media AS / Alamy; p.5 (CR): © Rrrainbow / Alamy; p.5 (CL): CBCK-Christine / Getty Images; p.5 (CB): © Nadiya Teslyuk / Alamy; p.5 (BR): © The Picture Pantry / Alamy; p.5 (BC): © Tetra Images / Alamy; p.5 (BL): © russ witherington / Alamy; p.5 (BC): © Tom Grundy / Alamy; p.5 (BR): © Tetra Images / Alamy; p.7 (TL): Kali Nine LLC / Getty Images; p.7 (BL): © Tetra Images / Alamy; p.7 (TR): Steve Smith / Getty Images; p.7 (CR): Marcus Mok / Getty Images; p.7 (BR): Hill Street Studios / Getty Images; p.8 (TL): Datacraft Co Ltd / Getty Images; p.8 (TR): © Archideaphoto / Alamy; p.8 (TL): © Zoonar GmbH / Alamy; p.8 (TR): © Dmitry Rukhlenko / Alamy; p.8 (TR): © aviv avivbenor / Alamy; p.8 (TL): Hemera Technologies / Getty Images; p.8 (CL): © Anton Starikov / Alamy; p.8 (CL): koya79 / Getty Images; p.8 (CL): © Héctor Sánchez / Alamy; p.8 (CR): © RTimages / Alamy; p.11 (BL): © Ivan Kmit / Alamy; p.11 (BL): © Robert Kneschke / Alamy; p.11 (BC): © Mark Sykes / Alamy; p.11 (BR): © Dmitry Rukhlenko / Alamy; p.11 (BR): © arkela / Alamy; p.13 (TR): © AHowden - Brazil Stock Photography / Alamy; p.13 (TL): © Cavan Images / Alamy; p.13 (BR): © Tiziana and Gianni Baldizzone/CORBIS; p.13 (BL): SensorSpot / Getty Images; p.15 (TR): © Action Plus Sports Images / Alamy; p.15 (TR): Jordi Ruiz / Getty Images; p.15 (TR): © infusny-244/INFphoto.com/ Corbis;p.15 (TR): © ROBIN UTRECHT FOTOGRAFIE/HillCreek Pictures/Corbis; p.15 (TR): Samir Hussein / Getty Images; p.19 (BR): Wavebreakmedia Ltd / Getty Images; p.20 (TC): JGI/Jamie Grill / Getty Images; p.20 (TL): © Sandra Baker / Alamy; p.20 (TL): KevinCarr / Getty Images; p.20 (TC): Alexander Hafemann / Getty Images; p.20 (TR): David Madison / Getty Images; p.20 (TR): © Jaak Nilson/Spaces Images/ Corbis; p.24 (TL): © ZUMA Press, Inc. / Alamy; p.24 (TR): Tom Hahn / Getty Images; p.24 (TC): © ZUMA Press, Inc. / Alamy; p.24 (TL): Mark Cunningham / MLB Photos via Getty Images; p.24 (TR): © Jason Smalley Photography / Alamy; p.26 (TL): Danita Delimont / Gallo Images / Getty Images; p.26 (TR): Rolf Hicker / Getty Images; p.26 (CL): © Robbie Jack/Corbis; p.26 (BR): © Janine Wiedel Photolibrary / Alamy; p.26 (BR): © Miles Davies / Alamy; p.26 (BL): Piotr Krzeslak / Shutterstock; p.27 (BL): © Hero Images/Corbis; p.27 (BR): © Phil Boorman/ Corbis; p.30 (TL): © BRETT GARDNER / Alamy; p.30 (TR): Amble Design / Shutterstock; p.30 (C): Wavebreak Premium / Shutterstock; p.30 (CR): © Blend Images / Alamy; p.31 (TL): AFP / Stringer / Getty Images; p.31 (TR): Mario Testino /Art Partner / Getty Images Publicity; p.31 (CR): © Peter Scholey / Alamy; p.32 (TL): © Denys Kuvaiev / Alamy; p.32 (TL): © Cavan Images / Alamy; p.32 (CL): © incamerastock / Alamy; p.32 (CL): © Gregg Vignal / Alamy; p.32 (BL): © Juice Images / Alamy; p.32 (BL): © Johner Images / Alamy; p.32 (CR): Jose Luis Pelaez Inc / Getty Images; p.32 (CR): JGI/Jamie Gril / Getty Images; p.32 (CR):

Hero Images / Getty Images; p.32 (CR): Jose Luis Pelaez Inc / Getty Images; p.32 (CR): Tanya Constantine / Getty Images; p.32 (CR): Maria Teijeiro / Getty Images; p.32 (CR): JGI/Jamie Grill; p.32 (CR): Streetfly Studio/JR Carvey / Getty Images; p.32 (CR): Jose Luis Pelaez Inc / Getty Images; p.35 (CL): sagir / Shutterstock; p.35 (CL): Fotovika / Shutterstock; p.35 (CL): Neamov / Shutterstock; p.35 (CL): © Maksym Bondarchuk / Alamy; p.35 (CL): © Yongyut Khasawaong / Alamy; p.35 (CL): © Stocksolutions / Alamy; p.35 (CL): Mosquito / DigitalVision Vectors / Getty Images; p.35 (CL): Rouzes / Getty Images; p.37 (CR): Westend61 / Getty Images; p.38 (BL): © imageBROKER / Alamy; p.38 (BL): © Helen Sessions / Alamy; p.38 (BR): © Robert Harding Picture Library Ltd / Alamy; p.38 (BR): © Dave G. Houser/Corbis; p.39 (TR): © imageBROKER / Alamy; p.39 (TC): © Felix Hug/Corbis; p.39 (BR): © Atlantide Phototravel/Corbis; p.42 (TL): © Gordon Shoosmith / Alamy; p.44 (TR): Roc Canals Photography / Getty Images; p.44 (TL): © CW Images / Alamy; p.44 (TR): © Krystyna Szulecka / Alamy; p.44 (TL): Insight Photography / Design Pic / Getty Images; p.44 (TL): © GerryRousseau / Alamy; p.44 (TC): © B. Leighty / Photri Images / Alamy; p.44 (CR): bluehand / Shutterstock; p.45 (CL): © Mira / Alamy; p.45 (B): © America / Alamy; p.48 (TL): © Auslöser/Corbis; p.48 (TR): Tara Moore / Getty Images; p.48 (BL): © mainpicture / Alamy; p.48 (BR): © Elvele Images Ltd / Alamy; p.48 (TL): Charlotte Nation / Getty Images; p.48 (BR): © redsnapper / Alamy; p.50 (TR): © David J. Green - Lifestyle / Alamy; p.50 (TR): Syda Productions / Shutterstock; p.50 (TR): Uwe Umstatter / Getty Images; p.50 (TR): Tetra Images / Getty Images; p.50 (TR): Blend Images - KidStock; p.50 (TR): Alex Segre / Getty Images; p.51 (TL): luismmolina / Getty Images; p.51 (TL): © RTimages / Alamy; p.51 (TL): Juffin / Getty Images; p.51 (TL): pictafolio / Getty Images; p.56 (TL): Avatar_023 / Getty Images; p.56 (TC): Peathegee Inc / Getty Images; p.56 (TR): © Hugh Sitton/ Corbis; p.56 (TR): © dbimages / Alamy; p.56 (C): © Keith Levit / Alamy; p.56 (C): Xavier Arnau / Getty Images; p.57 (T): Fuse / Getty Images; p.57 (L): Renee Eppler / Getty Images; p.57 (R): Stephan Kaps / EyeEm / Getty Images; p.59 (TR): Veena Nair / Getty Images; p.60 (TL): © Tetra Images / Alamy; p.60 (CR): © ZUMA Press, Inc. / Alamy; p.60 (CR): Jon Kopaloff / FilmMagic / Getty Images; p.60 (CR): Debby Wong / Shutterstock; p.60 (CR): Frederic Legrand - COMEO / Shutterstock; p.62 (TC): © ONOKY - Photononstop / Alamy; p.62 (TR): © Blaine Harrington III / Alamy; p.62 (C): © MELBA PHOTO AGENCY / Alamy; p.62 (C): Blend Images - Noel Hendrickson / Getty Images; p.61 (BL): Philip Game / Getty Images; p.61 (BC): © Craig Lovell / Eagle Visions Photography / Alamy; p.61 (BR): © Kim Steele/Blend Images / Corbis; p.64 (TR): Skip Odonnell / Getty Images; p.64 (BL): © Niels Poulsen / Alamy.

Commissioned photography by: Mike Stone p 18, 36, 54.

Cover photographs by: (L): ©Tim Gainey/Alamy Stock Photo; (R): ©Yuliya Koldovska/Shutterstock.

The publishers are grateful to the following illustrators:
Christos Skaltsas (hyphen) 4, 6, 9, 14, 15, 16, 17, 22, 23, 33, 34, 40, 43, 46, 52, 53, 55, 58, 60, 61 and Zaharias Papadopoulos (hyphen) 8, 12, 21, 35, 41, 63

The publishers are grateful to the following contributors: Hyphen: editorial, design, and project management; CityVox, LLC: audio recordings; Silversun Media Group: video production; Karen Elliott: Pronunciation sections; Matt Norton: Get it Right! sections

This page is intentionally left blank.

AMERICAN THiNK

WORKBOOK STARTER

A1

Herbert Puchta, Jeff Stranks & Peter Lewis-Jones

CAMBRIDGE
UNIVERSITY PRESS

This page is intentionally left blank.

CONTENTS

Welcome   4

WELCOME

The alphabet

1 🔊02 **Listen and write the names and the cities.**

Names

0 _Pedro_

1 _ _ _ _ _

2 _ _ _ _ _

3 _ _ _ _ _

4 _ _ _ _ _

5 _ _ _ _ _

Cities

1 _ _ _ _ _

2 _ _ _ _ _

3 _ _ _ _ _

4 _ _ _ _ _

5 _ _ _ _ _

6 _ _ _ _ _

2 **Match to make the words.**

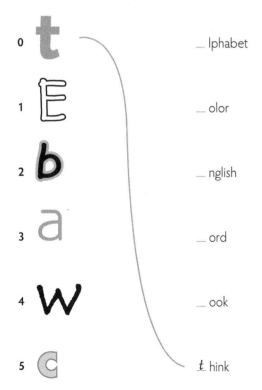

0 **t**   _ lphabet

1 **E**   _ olor

2 **b**   _ nglish

3 **a**   _ ord

4 **W**   _ ook

5 **C**   _t_ hink

Colors

1 🔊03 **Listen and write the colors. Then color.**

0 _black_   6 _ _ _ _

1 _ _ _ _   7 _ _ _ _

2 _ _ _ _   8 _ _ _ _

3 _ _ _ _   9 _ _ _ _

4 _ _ _ _   10 _ _ _ _

5 _ _ _ _

2 **Find and (circle) eleven colors in the word snake.**

greenorangeblackgraybluredpurplepinkbrownwhiteyellow

International words

1 Unscramble the letters to make words.

0 trapior *airport*

1 sub _____

2 facé _____

3 -fiiw _____

4 ishus _____

5 aaannb _____

6 rbumagerh _____

7 thole _____

8 iytc _____

9 openh _____

10 zizap _____

11 tranaurest _____

12 cinadswh _____

13 axit _____

14 inevilesto _____

15 bleatt _____

2 🔊 04 **Listen and put the words in order.**

a	☐	hamburger
b	☐	airport
c	☐	phone
d	☐	pizza
e	☐	café
f	☐	television
g	☐	tablet
h	1	sushi
i	☐	hotel
j	☐	city

SUMMING UP

1 🔊 05 **Listen and draw.**

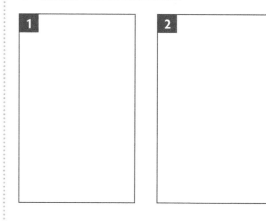

1	2
3	4
5	6

Articles: *a* and *an*

1 (Circle) the correct options.

0 *a /* (*an*) orange bus
1 *a / an* Italian city
2 *a / an* American TV show
3 *a / an* white tablet
4 *a / an* English actor
5 *a / an* hamburger
6 *a / an* black taxi
7 *a / an* phone
8 *a / an* gray house
9 *a / an* red bus

2 Write the words in the list in the correct columns. How many more words can you write?

~~actor~~ | airport | apple | city | hamburger
hotel | orange | TV show

a	an
	actor

The day

1 Look at the pictures and complete the phrases.

0 Good *m o r n i n g*   1 Good _ _ _ _ _ _

2 Good _ _ _ _ _ _ _ _   3 Good _ _ _ _ _ _ _ _ _

Saying *Hello* and *Goodbye*

1 Write the words in the list under the pictures.

Bye | Good afternoon | Good evening | Good morning | Good night | ~~Hello~~ | Hi | See you

_____*Hello*_____   _____   _____   _____

_____   _____   _____   _____

Classroom objects

1 Match the pictures with the words in the list. Write 1–10 in the boxes.

1 ~~book~~ | 2 chair | 3 computer | 4 desk
5 door | 6 pen | 7 pencil | 8 projector
9 board | 10 window

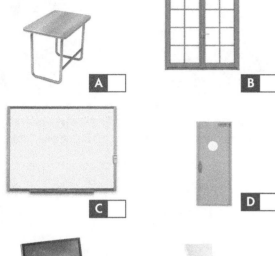

A B C D E F

G H

I J 1

2 Find the words from Exercise 1 in the word search.

```
W A B C Z B O A R D
I B R V N O W T O P
N O O R Q O M K T E
D P O T D K B L C N
O L D T B Z K S E D
W N V M I Q G J J U
E S R E T U P M O C
X J L V C H A I R Z
L R F L I C N E P M
G S Y H X E K L Q B
```

SUMMING UP

1 🔊06 Put the dialogues in order. Then listen and check.

Dialogue 1

☐1 CONNOR — Good morning, Mr. Davis.
☐ CONNOR — I'm fine. And you?
☐ MR. DAVIS — Hello, Connor. How are you?
☐ MR. DAVIS — I'm great, thanks.

Dialogue 2

☐ LUCAS — Yeah, have a good day.
☐ LUCAS — Bye, Paula.
☐ PAULA — Bye, Lucas. See you later.

Dialogue 3

☐ LILY — I'm fine, thank you.
☐ LILY — Bye, Mrs. Edwards.
☐ LILY — Good afternoon, Mrs. Edwards.
☐ MRS. EDWARDS — Good. I'll see you in class.
☐ MRS. EDWARDS — Hello, Lily. How are you?

2 Write dialogues.

OLIVIA — *Hello.* ___
JIM — ___
BRIAN — ___
OLIVIA — ___

TIM — ___
DAD — ___

7

Numbers 0–20

1 Write the numbers in the boxes.

1	four	`4`	12	seven	
2	eight		13	sixteen	
3	twenty		14	eighteen	
4	five		15	ten	
5	twelve		16	fourteen	
6	six		17	three	
7	eleven		18	thirteen	
8	one		19	seventeen	
9	fifteen		20	two	
10	nineteen		21	nine	
11	zero				

Plural nouns

1 How many? Find, count, and write the plurals.

book | chair | child | computer | door | ~~man~~
pencil | pen | phone | window | woman

0	eight	*men*
1	three	
2	seven	
3	fifteen	
4	eighteen	
5	two	
6	one	
7	zero	
8	twelve	
9	four	
10	six	

Classroom language

1 (Circle) the correct options.

0   *Close your books. /*
    What does this mean?

1   *Raise your hand. /*
    Close your books.

2   *Listen. /*
    That's right.

3   *Work with a partner. /*
    That's wrong.

4   *Listen. /*
    Look at the picture.

5   *Work with a partner. /*
    Raise your hand.

6   *Open your books. /*
    Look at the picture.

Numbers 20–100

1 Write the numbers.

0	seventy	70
1	thirty	
2	forty	
3	ninety	
4	one hundred	
5	fifty	
6	twenty	
7	sixty	
8	eighty	
9	thirty-four	
10	sixty-eight	
11	twenty-one	
12	ninety-nine	
13	fifty-three	

2 ◀))07 Listen and write the numbers.

0	*thirty-four*
1	
2	
3	
4	
5	
6	
7	
8	
9	
10	
11	
12	
13	
14	

Messages

1 ◀))08 Listen to the messages and (circle) the correct options.

Message 1

Hi, Luke

Message from Paul [1] Jones / James.
His address is [2] 7 / 8 Elm Street.
The bus number is [3] 8 / 9.
His phone number is
[4] 298-555-8758 / 298-555-6758.

Message 2

Hi, Debbie

Message from [5] Claire / Clare [6] Green / Greene.
Her address is [7] 44 / 34 Park Lane.
The bus number is [8] 15 / 16.
Her phone number is
[9] 237-564-1453 / 237-563-1453.

SUMMING UP

1 ◀))09 Listen and complete the messages.

Message 1

Hi, Marco

Message from Mr. [0] *Cleverly*.
His address is [1] _____ Valley Street.
The bus number is [2] _____.
His phone number is [3] _____

Message 2

Hi, Carla

Message from Jane [4] _____.
Her address is [5] _____ Ridge Road.
The bus number is [6] _____.
Her phone number is [7] _____

GRAMMAR
Question words `SB page 14`

1 ★☆☆ Complete the sentences with the correct question words.

> 0 **What** 's your name?

> 1 _____ old are you?

> 2 _____ are you from?

> 3 _____ is your favorite sportsperson?

> 4 _____ is he/she your favorite?

2 ★★★ Write answers to the questions in Exercise 1 so they are true for you.

0 *My name is* _____
1 _____
2 _____
3 _____
4 _____

Pronunciation
/h/ or /w/ in question words
Go to page 118. 🔊

---

3 ★★☆ Look at the pictures and circle the correct words.

0 *He /* She */ It* is happy.

1 *We / You / I* are friends.

2 *They / We / You* are Japanese.

3 *She / He / It* is 11.

4 *I / She / We* am Carla.

5 *We / They / You* are Josh.

6 *We / You / They* are sisters.

7 *I / It / You* is the Brazilian flag.

The verb *be* SB page 15

4 ★ ☆ ☆ **Complete the table with the words in the list.**

am | are | are | are | is | is | is

0	I	*am*	Paul.
1	You		13.
2	He		happy.
3	She		from Mexico.
4	It		Japanese.
5	We		sisters.
6	They		friends.

5 ★★ ☆ **Complete the sentences with the verb *be*. Use short forms.**

0 You *'re* _____ Russian.

1 I _____ Portuguese.

2 We _____ Mexican.

3 They _____ Brazilian.

4 He _____ Australian.

6 ★★ ☆ **Rewrite the sentences using short forms.**

0 It is a Turkish flag.
   It's a Turkish flag.

1 She is Russian.
   _____

2 You are a good friend.
   _____

3 They are British.
   _____

4 We are from Boston.
   _____

5 I am Paul. What is your name?
   _____

6 He is 12 today.
   _____

5 She _____ American.

GET IT RIGHT!

Subject–verb agreement with *be*

We use the form of *be* that agrees with the subject.

✓ *They **are** from Italy.*

✗ *They is from Italy.*

Correct the sentences.

0 There are a beautiful beach.
   There is a beautiful beach.

1 The classes two hours long.
   _____

2 It are cold today.
   _____

3 Are the English player good?
   _____

4 We's from France.
   _____

5 My favorite country are the U.S.
   _____

VOCABULARY

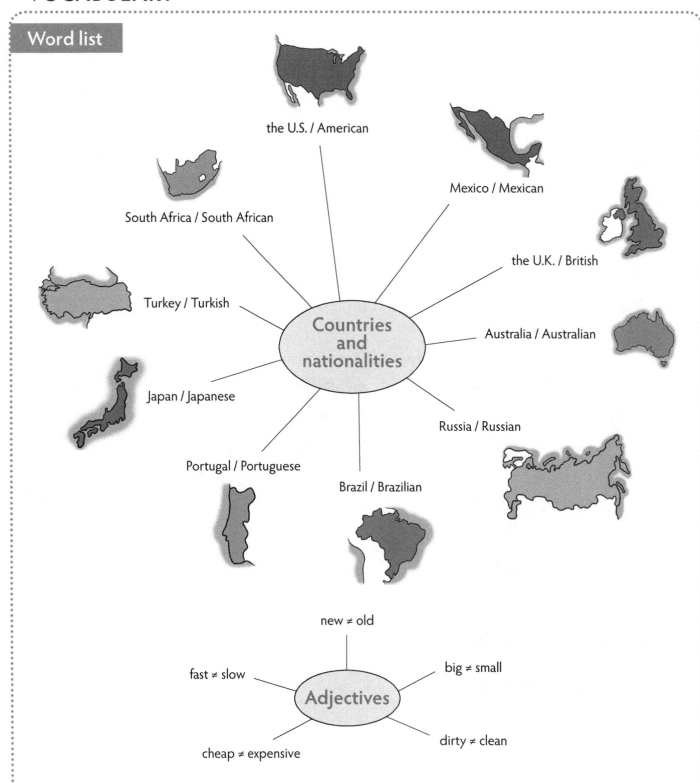

the U.S. / American

Mexico / Mexican

South Africa / South African

the U.K. / British

Turkey / Turkish

Countries and nationalities

Australia / Australian

Japan / Japanese

Russia / Russian

Portugal / Portuguese

Brazil / Brazilian

new ≠ old

fast ≠ slow

big ≠ small

Adjectives

dirty ≠ clean

cheap ≠ expensive

Key words in context

country	Mexico is a beautiful **country**.
fan	I'm a big **fan** of Jennifer Lawrence.
flag	The American **flag** is red, white, and blue.
nationality	What's your **nationality**?
player	Gareth Bale is my favorite soccer **player**.
sportsperson	Usain Bolt is a famous **sportsperson** from Jamaica.

Countries and nationalities
SB page 14

1 ★☆☆ **Find ten countries in the word search. Then write the countries.**

G	H	I	S	O	C	I	X	E	M
U	B	R	A	Z	I	L	S	G	E
A	B	V	J	A	S	K	O	J	T
I	C	N	A	M	P	S	U	I	U
L	Y	E	I	F	A	L	T	C	R
A	M	Z	S	E	F	L	H	G	K
R	T	B	S	K	R	R	A	H	E
T	H	E	U	S	A	U	F	X	Y
S	E	V	R	W	T	Z	R	B	J
U	U	J	A	P	A	N	I	T	Q
A	K	K	A	Y	H	B	C	N	M
G	P	O	R	T	U	G	A	L	D

0   *Brazil*

1   _____

2   _____

3   _____

4   _____

5   _____

6   _____

7   _____

8   _____

9   _____

2 ★★☆ **Complete the words.**

0   Oliver's from Cape Town. He's South Afric *an* .

1   He's from London. He's Briti_____ .

2   I'm from Mexico City. I'm Mexic_____ .

3   She's from New York. She's Americ_____ .

4   They're from Sydney. They're Australi_____ .

5   You're from Moscow. You're Russi_____ .

6   My mom is from Rio. She's Brazili_____ .

7   Our teacher is from Lisbon. He's Portugu_____ .

8   Ryoko is from Tokyo. She's Japan_____ .

9   They're from Istanbul. They're Turk_____ .

Adjectives
SB page 17

3 ★☆☆ **Write the adjectives under the pictures.**

big | cheap | clean | dirty | ~~expensive~~
fast | new | old | slow | small

The car is …

0   *expensive* .

1   _____ .

2   _____ .

3   _____ .

4   _____ .

The car is …

5   _____ .

6   _____ .

7   _____ .

8   _____ .

9   _____ .

4 ★★☆ **Put the words in order to make sentences.**

0   book / English / My / new / is

   My English book is new.

1   red / Her / is / pen

   _____

2   is / house / old / Our

   _____

3   fast / bikes / Their / are

   _____

4   big / school / Our / is

   _____

5   My / small / bedroom / is

   _____

6   car / Her / expensive / is

   _____

READING

1 REMEMBER AND CHECK Complete the table. Then look at the website on page 13 of the Student's Book and check your answers.

Name	Age	Country	City	Favorite sportsperson
Pedro	10			
Brittany				
Oleg				
Yumi				

2 Read the text quickly. Where are they from? Match the names with the countries.

0 Juan   [c]   a Turkey
1 Mary Lynn   [ ]   b South Africa
2 Ibrahim   [ ]   c Mexico
3 Rebecca   [ ]   d the U.S.
4 Lucy   [ ]   e the U.K.

Hi, my name's Juan. I'm from Acapulco. I'm Mexican. I'm 12 years old.
My favorite sportsperson is James Rodriguez. He's a soccer player from Colombia. He's great.

My name's Mary Lynn. I'm 10 years old. I'm American. I'm from Dallas.
My favorite sportsperson is Rafael Nadal. He's a tennis player. He's Spanish. He's awesome.

Hi, I'm Ibrahim. I'm from Istanbul. I'm Turkish. I'm 11 years old.
My favorite sportsperson is Ellie Simmonds. She's a swimmer from the U.K. She's really fast.

My name's Rebecca. I'm 12 years old. I'm South African. I'm from Cape Town.
My favorite sportsperson is Marta. She's a soccer player. She's Brazilian. She's amazing.

My name's Lucy. I'm 11 years old. I'm British. I'm from Liverpool.
My favorite sportsperson is Usain Bolt. He's a runner. He's Jamaican. He's a great athlete.

3 Read the text again. Mark the sentences T (true) or F (false).

0 Juan is from Mexico City.   [F]
1 Juan's favorite sportsperson is a soccer player.   [ ]
2 Mary Lynn is 10.   [ ]
3 Mary Lynn's favorite sportsperson is a Brazilian tennis player. [ ]
4 Ibrahim is from Turkey.   [ ]
5 Ellie Simmonds is an American swimmer.   [ ]
6 Rebecca is 11.   [ ]
7 Rebecca is from Brazil.   [ ]
8 Lucy is from Liverpool.   [ ]
9 Lucy's favorite sportsperson is a woman.   [ ]

DEVELOPING WRITING

About me

1 Read the questionnaire. Then complete the text with the missing words.

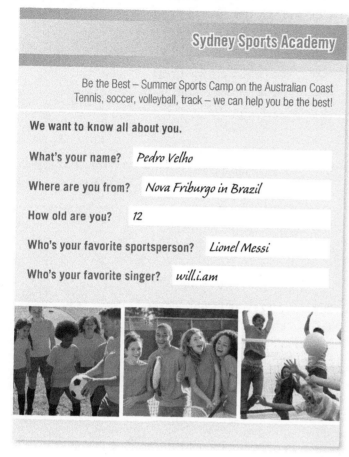

Sydney Sports Academy

Be the Best – Summer Sports Camp on the Australian Coast
Tennis, soccer, volleyball, track – we can help you be the best!

We want to know all about you.

What's your name? *Pedro Velho*

Where are you from? *Nova Friburgo in Brazil*

How old are you? *12*

Who's your favorite sportsperson? *Lionel Messi*

Who's your favorite singer? *will.i.am*

Hi, my name is ⁰___ *Pedro* ___.
I'm Brazilian. I'm from ¹_____.
I'm ²_____ years old.
My favorite sportsperson is
³_____.
He's a soccer player from Argentina.
He's amazing. I love soccer!
I love music, too. My favorite singer is
⁴_____. He's awesome.

2 Use the text to complete the questionnaire.

Sydney Sports Academy

Be the Best – Summer Sports Camp on the Australian Coast
Tennis, soccer, volleyball, track – we can help you be the best!

We want to know all about you.

Hi, my name is Amy Davies. I'm American.
I'm from Seattle. I'm 11 years old.
My favorite sportsperson is Serena
Williams. She's a tennis player from the
U.S. She's awesome. I love tennis!
I love music, too. My favorite singer is
Taylor Swift. She's great.

What's your name? ⁰ *Amy Davies*

Where are you from? ¹_____

How old are you? ²_____

Who's your favorite sportsperson? ³_____

Who's your favorite singer? ⁴_____

3 Complete the text about you.

Hi, my name is ¹_____ . I'm ²_____ .
I'm from ³_____ . I'm ⁴_____ years old. My favorite
sportsperson is ⁵_____ . She/He's a ⁶_____
from ⁷_____ . She/He's ⁸_____ . I love ⁹
_____ ! I love music, too. My favorite singer is ¹⁰_____ .
She/He's ¹¹_____ .

LISTENING

1 🔊 12 **Listen to the dialogue. Number the people in the order you hear them.**

[ ]

[0]

[ ]

[ ]

[ ]

2 🔊 12 **Listen again and write the names in the list under the pictures in Exercise 1.**

Ayse | Haruka | Kayla | Roberto | Steve

3 Circle **the correct answers (A or B).**

0 Haruka is from …
   (A) Tokyo.   B Lisbon.
1 Roberto is from …
   A Tokyo.   B Lisbon.
2 Ayse is from …
   A Istanbul.   B Moscow.
3 Steve is from …
   A London.   B Cape Town.
4 Kayla is from …
   A London.   B Cape Town.

DIALOGUE

Choose the correct answers (A, B, or C) to complete the dialogue.

BOY   Hi. What's your name?
GIRL 0 A I'm 12.
         B Brazil.
         (C) Julia.

BOY   And where are you from?
GIRL 1 A I'm American.
         B I'm 10.
         C Sara.

BOY   What city are you from?
GIRL 2 A Japan.
         B New York.
         C Brazil.

BOY   New York's a beautiful city.
GIRL 3 A Yes, I am.
         B Yes, it is.
         C Yes, they are.

BOY   Who's your favorite singer?
GIRL 4 A Pharrell Williams.
         B Ronaldo.
         C Yes.

BOY   Why is he your favorite singer?
GIRL 5 A No.
         B Yes.
         C Because he's awesome.

BOY   Nice to meet you, Julia.
GIRL 6 A Yes.
         B No.
         C Nice to meet you, too.

PHRASES FOR FLUENCY

1 Match the phrases 1–4 with their similar meanings a–d.

1 How's it going?   [ ]   a Goodbye.
2 See you later.   [ ]   b How are you?
3 I know!   [ ]   c Great.
4 That is so awesome! [ ]   d You're right.

2 Use the phrases 1–4 in Exercise 1 to complete the mini-dialogues.

1 A Hi, Mark. _____
   B Fine, thanks.

2 A Bye, Jen.
   B Bye, Tim. _____

3 A This is my new laptop.
   B _____

4 A John's a great soccer player.
   B _____

Sum it up

The Big World Quiz

1 **Where do you find these things?**

1

A Japan
B the U.K.
C Spain

3

A Mexico
B Brazil
C Japan

2

A the U.S.
B Turkey
C Russia

4

A the U.K.
B Portugal
C South Africa

2 **Where do they say "hello" like this?**

1 "How's it going?"
  A the U.S.
  B Portugal
  C Brazil
2 "Buenos dias"
  A Mexico
  B Turkey
  C the U.K.
3 "Konnichiwa"
  A Russia
  B South Africa
  C Japan
4 "Merhaba"
  A Russia
  B Turkey
  C Mexico

3 **Where are these capital cities?**

1 Lisbon
  A Portugal
  B Brazil
  C Mexico
2 Pretoria
  A the U.K.
  B Japan
  C South Africa
3 Ankara
  A the U.S.
  B Turkey
  C Australia
4 Brasilia
  A Mexico
  B Russia
  C Brazil

4 **Who is from ...**

1 Brazil?
  A Marta
  B Tony Kroos
  C James Rodriguez
2 the U.K.?
  A Serena Williams
  B Usain Bolt
  C Ellie Simonds
3 Russia?
  A Bruno Mars
  B Maria Sharapova
  C will.i.am
4 the U.S.?
  A Taylor Swift
  B Gareth Bale
  C Lionel Messi

2 | I FEEL HAPPY

GRAMMAR

be (singular and plural, negative)
SB page 22

1 ★☆☆ (Circle) the correct form of *be*.

0 Joe (is)/ *am* happy today. It *'s* / *'re* his birthday.

1 We *am* / *are* excited. We *'s* / *'re* on vacation.

2 It *'s* / *'m* late. I *'s* / *'m* tired.

3 Helen and Amanda *is* / *are* happy today. They *is* / *are* on the tennis team.

4 You *are* / *is* angry.

5 It *is* / *are* hot here.

2 ★★☆ Complete the sentences with the correct negative form of *be*.

0 I *'m not* tired. I'm worried.

1 Jack _____ happy. He's bored.

2 Carla and Jane _____ worried. They're excited.

3 We _____ angry with you. We're worried about you. That's all.

4 Susan _____ happy at her new school. Her new classmates _____ very friendly.

5 It _____ hot in here. It's cold. Close the window.

6 I _____ hungry. I'm thirsty.

be (questions and short answers)
SB page 23

3 ★★☆ (Circle) the correct form of *be*.

0 A *Is* I (Are) Chris and Matt with you?
  B No, they *isn't* / *aren't*.

1 A *Am* / *Is* I on your team?
  B Yes, you *is* / *are*.

2 A *Am* / *Are* you at the beach now?
  B No, we *isn't* / *aren't*.

3 A *Is* / *Are* Nick at home?
  B No, he *isn't* / *aren't*.

4 A *Is* / *Are* Emma at school today?
  B Yes, she *is* / *are*.

5 A *Am* / *Are* you American?
  B No, I *'m not* / *aren't*.

4 ★★☆ Write the questions. Then write answers to the questions so they are true for you.

0 your name / Maria?
  Is your name Maria?   *No, it isn't.*

1 you / 15?
  _____   _____

2 you / Mexican?
  _____   _____

3 your mom / a teacher?
  _____   _____

4 your dad / from Brazil?
  _____   _____

5 you / happy?
  _____   _____

6 your / classmates / friendly?
  _____   _____

5 ★★☆ Complete the text messages with the correct form of *be*.

Hi, Kathy, 0 ___*Are*___ you happy?
1 _____ your new school OK?
2 _____ the students friendly?
3 _____ it sunny there? It
4 _____ (✗) sunny here ☹.
School 5 _____ (✗) the same without you ☹. Text me.

Hi, Lauren, I 6 _____ (✓) happy ☺.
School 7 _____ (✓) very different here in Australia. There 8 _____ (✓)
10 boys and 12 girls in my class.
The girls 9 _____ (✓) very friendly, but the boys 10 _____
11 _____ (✗) ☹. It _____ (✓) very hot and sunny here ☺. And guess what? There
12 _____ (✓) a swimming pool in the schoolyard ☺. It 13 _____ (✗) all bad!

Object pronouns `SB page 25`

6 ★ ☆ ☆ **Complete the sentences with *me*, *him*, *her*, *us*, *you*, and *them*.**

My new school

0 My new school is excellent. I really like
____*it*____ .

1 The school lunches are great. I like _____ .

2 Our English teacher is Mrs. Santos. I like
_____ .

3 We are good students. Mrs. Santos is very happy
with _____ .

4 Tim is my best friend here. He's great. I really like
_____ .

5 I'm friendly. My classmates like _____ .

6 Are you friendly? Do your classmates like
_____ ?

7 ★★ ☆ **Complete the dialogues so they are true for
you. Use the correct object pronouns.**

0 A Do you like ___*Neymar*___ ? (sportsperson)

 B Yes, I really like ____*him*____ .

1 A Do you like _____ ? (girl singer)

 B Yes, I like _____ . She's great.

2 A Do you like _____ ? (pop group)

 B No, I don't like _____ . They're terrible.

3 A Do you like _____ ? (actor)

 B Yes, I like _____ . He's an excellent actor.

4 A Do you like _____ ? (movie)

 B Yes, I like _____ . It's very funny.

8 ★★★ **Write questions with *like* and the word in
parentheses. Then write answers to the questions
so they are true for you.**

0 Katy Perry? (you)

 Do you like Katy Perry?

 Yes, I like her. She's a great singer.

1 the TV show *Dr Who*? (you)

 _____

 _____

2 soccer? (your dad)

 _____

 _____

3 the band called The Asteroids Galaxy Tour? (your
best friend)

 _____

 _____

4 Taylor Swift? (you)

 _____

 _____

5 comedy movies? (your mom)

 _____

 _____

6 the song "Good Feeling" by Flo Rida? (you)

 _____

 _____

7 talent shows? (your mom and dad)

 _____

 _____

GET IT RIGHT!

Object pronouns

We use *it* in the singular and *them* in the plural

✓ *I don't want this book. You can have **it**.*

✓ *I don't want these books. You can have **them**.*

✗ *I don't want these books. You can have **it**.*

(Circle) **the correct options.**

0 This is my school. I like (it) / them.

1 I play computer games. I like *it* / *them*.

2 My dad has a really cool phone. I want *it* / *them*!

3 My house is small, but I like *it* / *them* a lot.

4 The Black Keys? I don't like *it* / *them*.

5 My friends are here. I play football with *it* / *them*
every afternoon.

6 Here is my homework. I finished *it* / *them* this
morning.

VOCABULARY

Adjectives to describe feelings

cold

hot

hungry

thirsty

sad

worried

excited

bored

angry

tired

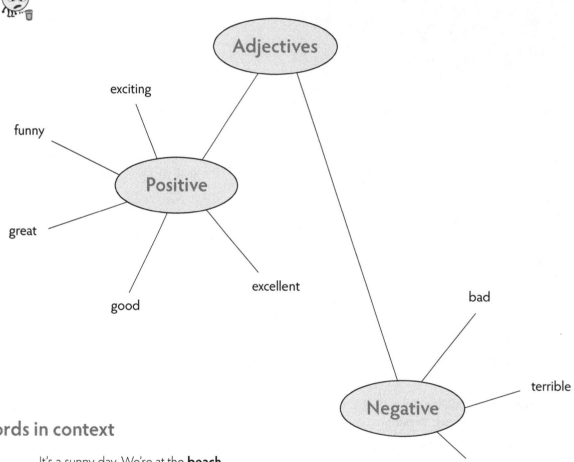

Adjectives

Positive
- exciting
- funny
- great
- good
- excellent

Negative
- bad
- terrible
- awful

Key words in context

beach	It's a sunny day. We're at the **beach**.
bus	I'm on the **bus** with my friends.
candy	I like chocolate and **candy**.
club	It's a youth **club**. They have lots of different things to do there.
friendly	I like Kate. She's very **friendly**.
mask	My mom's carnival **mask** is very beautiful.
movie	I like comedy **movies**. They're funny.
song	I love the **song** "Royals" by Lorde.
stadium	I'm at the **stadium**. There's a baseball game today.
team	Mike is on our soccer **team**.
train	We're on the **train** with my mom.
vacation	My friend is on **vacation** in Australia.

Adjectives to describe feelings
SB page 22

1 ★☆☆ **Unscramble the letters to make adjectives.**

0 r e d i t *tired*

1 x c e t i e d _ _ _ _ _ _ _

2 o r r w i e d _ _ _ _ _ _ _

3 y a n g r _ _ _ _ _

4 o r b e d _ _ _ _ _

5 o h t _ _ _

6 s t y i r t h _ _ _ _ _ _

7 d a s _ _ _

8 d l o c _ _ _ _

9 g r y n u h _ _ _ _ _ _

2 ★★☆ **Complete the sentences with the adjectives in Exercise 1.**

0 It's late and you're ___*tired*___ . Go to bed.

1 My new bike is broken. My dad's _____ with me.

2 I'm _____ . Let's play a game on your tablet.

3 My friends are _____ . There's a soccer game at our school today.

4 Ethan is _____ about the big test today.

5 Andy's dog is sick. He's _____ .

6 I'm hot and _____ . Can I have a drink?

7 He's _____ . He wants a sandwich.

8 It's winter. It's _____ .

9 We're _____ . Let's go for a swim!

3 ★★★ (Circle) **the correct adjectives.**

0 A Are you (worried) / excited about the exam tomorrow?
   B No, I'm not. It's an easy exam.

1 A Is Kate excited / bored about vacation?
   B Yes, she is.

2 A It's cold / hot today. Let's go swimming.
   B Yes, OK. That's a good idea.

3 A Are you hungry / thirsty?
   B Yes, I am.
   A Let's have some pizza then.

4 A It's really hot / cold in here.
   B You're right. Let's close the window.

5 A I'm really tired / thirsty.
   B Here's a bottle of water.
   A Thanks.

6 A Mom's angry / sad with you.
   B Why?
   A You're very late.

Positive and negative adjectives
SB page 25

4 ★★☆ **Unscramble the words and complete the sentences.**

0 He's a ___*bad*___ actor. (dba)

1 She's a _____ player. (ogod)

2 São Paulo is a _____ city. (arget)

3 The weather today is _____ . (fluwa)

4 It's a _____ show. (unfyn)

5 This movie isn't good. It's _____ ! (ritlerbe)

6 The pizzas here are _____ . (etncxelle)

7 Volleyball is an _____ sport. (igecntix)

5 ★☆☆ **Complete the sentences so they are true for you.**

0 ___*Shakira*___ is a great singer.

1 _____ is a good book.

2 _____ is a funny actor.

3 _____ is a terrible sport.

4 _____ is a great soccer player.

5 _____ is an exciting city.

6 _____ is an awful computer game.

7 _____ is a bad song.

8 _____ and _____ are excellent games.

6 ★★☆ **Complete the dialogues so they are true for you. Use Yes, I do or No, I don't and an adjective from the list.**

awful | bad | excellent | exciting
funny | good | ~~great~~ | terrible

0 A Do you like soccer?
   B ___*Yes, I do*___ . It's (a)/an ___*great*___ sport.

1 A Do you like swimming?
   B _____ . It's a/an _____ sport.

2 A Do you like the Harry Potter books?
   B _____ . They're _____ books.

3 A Do you like basketball?
   B _____ . It's a/an _____ game.

4 A Do you like Carlos Sanchez?
   B _____ . He's a/an _____ soccer player.

5 A Do you like The Hobbit movies?
   B _____ . They're _____ movies.

Pronunciation
Vowel sounds: adjectives
Go to page 118.

READING

1 REMEMBER AND CHECK Complete the sentences with *likes* or *doesn't like*. Then look at the dialogue on page 24 of the Student's Book and check your answers.

0 Nick *doesn't like* baseball.
1 Ethan _____ Ben Stiller.
2 Nick _____ him.
3 Nick _____ Maroon 5.
4 Nick _____ ice cream.
5 Nick _____ Jen Carter.

2 Read the profile of a famous singer quickly. Find and <u>underline</u> the answers to these questions.

1 What's her real name?
2 What's her stage name?

Name: Ella Yelich-O'Connor
Stage Name: Lorde
Nationality: New Zealander
Place of Birth: New Zealand
Likes: photography, music, and books

The year is 2013. Ella Yelich-O'Connor is in high school. She's a 16-year-old teenager from New Zealand. Her mother's name is Sonja Yelich, and she's Croatian. Her father's name is Vic O'Connor, and he's Irish. Ella is a famous singer, and her hit "Royals" is at the top of the New Zealand charts. Her first album is in the top five in the U.K., Canada, the U.S., Ireland, and Norway. Maybe it's a hit in your country, too! Ella Yelich-O'Connor is a queen of pop music. She likes electronic music, too, and she really likes hip hop.

She's a style icon but does she like fashion?
Yes, she does. She loves clothes.

Does she like social media?
Yes, she does. She likes Twitter and Instagram.

What does she like?
Ella likes books – all kinds of books. Books are important to her. The words of her songs are from books, and her songs are like short stories.

3 Read the profile again and write short answers to the questions.

0 Is her stage name Ella? _No, it isn't._
1 Does she like photography? _____
2 Is Lorde from New York? _____
3 Is her father Irish? _____
4 Is she a singer? _____
5 Does she like electronic music? _____
6 Does she like clothes? _____
7 Are books important to her? _____
8 Is she popular in your country? _____

DEVELOPING WRITING

A text message

1 Read the text messages and <u>underline</u> the adjectives.

a

Hi, Amy. Are you still bored? Read a book! My favorite is *Anne of Green Gables*. It's a great book. I really like Anne. She's friendly and funny. It's a happy story ☺. Please read it.
Kate

b

Hey, Matt. I'm at the movies. The movie is terrible. I don't like it. The actors are very bad. I don't like them. I'm really bored ☹. Where are you? Text me.
Tim

c

Hi, James. Are you at home? Listen to this song. It's great. The singer is excellent. The guitarist is good. I really like the song. Do you like it? Text me.
Lara

d

Hi, Sally. Thank you for the movie. I really like it. My sister likes it, too.
Jim Carrey is great. He's a very funny actor. The other actors are good, too. Speak soon.
Hannah

e

Hi, Tony. The song is terrible. The singer is awful. How is it number 1? I don't like it. My friends don't like it. Do you like it?
Jake

2 Write the adjectives in Exercise 1 in the correct columns.

Positive	Negative
	bored

3 Look at the text messages in Exercise 1. Use *likes* or *doesn't like* to complete the sentences.

0 Kate ____*likes*____ the book. It's a ___*happy*___ story.
1 Tim _____ the movie. It's _____ .
2 Lara _____ the singer. He's _____ .
3 Hannah _____ Jim Carrey. He's _____ .
4 Jake _____ the song. It's _____ .

4 You like a book and you want to text a friend about it. Complete the text message.

Hi, _____ . Are you still bored? Read a book! My favorite is _____ . It's a _____ book. I really like _____ . He/She is _____ . It's a _____ story. Please read it.

5 You don't like a movie and you want to text a friend about it. Complete the text message.

Hey _____ . I'm at the movies. The movie is _____ . I _____ it. The actors are _____ . I _____ them. I'm really _____ ☹. Where are you? Text me.

6 Think about a movie, a book, a band, or a song and write notes about it in your notebook.

Title: _____
like / don't like   great / terrible
_____
_____
_____

7 Now write a short text message about the movie, book, band, or song. Write 35–50 words.

LISTENING

1 🔊 15 **Listen to the dialogues. Which dialogue (1–5) matches the photo?**

2 🔊 15 **Listen again and mark the sentences T (true) or F (false).**

1 It's Emma's birthday. `T`
2 Tom is cold. ☐
3 John doesn't like English. ☐
4 Tim doesn't like the movie. ☐
5 Helen's cat is sick. ☐

3 🔊 15 **Listen again and ⟨circle⟩ the correct options.**

1 **A** Hi, Jane.
 B Oh, hi, Kate.
 A It's Emma's birthday today. Is she *happy* / ⟨*excited*⟩?
 B Yes, she is. I'm *happy* / *excited*, too.

2 **A** What's wrong?
 B It's *hot* / *cold* in here. Are you *hot* / *cold*, Tom?
 A *No, I'm not.* / *Yes, I am.* I'm wearing a sweater.
 B Well, I'm very *hot* / *cold*. Can you *open* / *close* the window?
 A OK.

3 **A** There's a test tomorrow. Are you worried, John?
 B No, I'm not worried about it. I *like* / *don't like* English. I'm just tired.
 A Well, I'm worried. I'm very worried. I *like* / *don't like* English.

4 **A** What's wrong, Tim? Are you *tired* / *bored*?
 B No, I'm not. I'm just *tired* / *bored*. I don't like this movie.
 A Why? I *like* / *don't like* it. It's very funny.

5 **A** What's wrong with Helen? Why is she *sad* / *angry*?
 B Her cat's sick. It's at the vet's.
 A Oh, no. That's *terrible* / *exciting*. Poor Helen.

DIALOGUE

Complete the dialogue with the words in the list.

don't like | funny | great | ~~likes~~
likes | terrible

A Do you like the song "Let It Go" from the movie *Frozen*?
B No, I don't. But my little sister ⁰____*likes*____ it. It's her favorite song. She sings it all the time. In fact, she ¹_____ all the songs from the movie.
A Do you like the movie?
B No, I don't. It's ²_____ . I ³_____ animated movies.
A Well, I really like it. It's a ⁴_____ movie. It's ⁵_____ .

▰▰ TRAIN TO THINK ▰▰

Categorizing

1 **Put the words in the list into categories. There are four words for each category.**

~~beach~~ | ~~Brazil~~ | ~~cold~~ | New Zealand | sad
school | stadium | the U.S. | theater | thirsty
tired | Turkey

Countries	Feelings	Places
Brazil	*cold*	*beach*

2 **Put words in these three categories.**

Nationalities	Colors	Classroom things
American		

3 **Name the categories.**

1	2	3
good	fourteen	Lara
great	sixty-three	Tim
terrible	one hundred	Kate

Skimming

Reading tip

- Read the questions first. Then read the text quickly.
- Think about what type of text it is. Is it a newspaper article? A letter or an email? A text message?
- Underline the "important" words, such as adjectives, nouns, and verbs.
- Try to answer *Wh-* questions – *Who*, *What*, *When*, and *Where*.

1 Read the questions under the text in Exercise 5 quickly. Who is the text about (mostly)?

  A Henry Hunter

  B Samantha

  C Samantha's brother

2 Skim the text in Exercise 5. What type is it?

  A a newspaper article

  B an email

  C a text message

3 Find and write these "important" words from the text.

two emotions

_____

_____

two positive adjectives

_____

_____

two negative adjectives

_____

_____

4 Complete the table with information about the text.

Who?	
What?	
When?	
Where?	

5 Read the text again and choose the correct answers (A or B).

Hi, Tess,

I'm bored. It's my little brother Tim's birthday today. He's eight. He's very excited. All his friends are here. It's hot and sunny. They're in the yard now. His friends from his school soccer team are here. So of course, they all like soccer. His favorite team is Chelsea. I like Chelsea, too. They're an excellent team.

Guess what his gift from me is? It's a Chelsea soccer ball! Oh, and a book – *Henry Hunter and the Beast of Snagon*. It's a great story, and I really like the pictures. They're excellent.

His gifts from Mom and Dad are a bike and a DVD. It's a really good bike, but the movie is terrible. It's called *Dumb and Dumber*. I don't like it. It isn't funny ☹.

It's 11 a.m. – Tim's birthday lunch is in an hour. But I'm hungry now. There's a big birthday cake ☺.

See you soon,

Samantha

0 Is Samantha excited?

  A Yes, she is.

  (B) No, she isn't.

1 Is it her brother's birthday today?

  A Yes, it is.

  B No, it isn't.

2 Is it a hot day?

  A Yes, it is.

  B No, it isn't.

3 Samantha _____ Chelsea.

  A likes

  B doesn't like

4 *Henry Hunter and the Beast of Snagon* is a/an _____ book.

  A awful

  B great

5 Samantha doesn't like the *Dumb and Dumber* movies. They _____ funny.

  A are

  B aren't

6 Is Samantha thirsty?

  A Yes, she is.

  B No, she isn't.

CONSOLIDATION

LISTENING

1 🔊16 **Listen to Annie and (circle) the correct answers (A, B, or C).**

1 Annie is from …

A   the U.S.

B   South Africa

C   Mexico

2 She's …

    A   12.   B   13.   C   14.

3 Her best friend is from …

A   Brazil

B   South Africa

C   the U.K.

4 Her best friend is named …

    A   Paulo.

    B   Pedro.

    C   Mario.

2 🔊16 **Listen again and mark the sentences T (true) or F (false).**

1 Annie is from Cape Town. ☐

2 She doesn't like sports. ☐

3 Her favorite sportsperson is a tennis player. ☐

4 Her favorite singer is Taylor Swift. ☐

5 Her best friend is Spanish. ☐

6 Her best friend is the same age as her. ☐

VOCABULARY

3 **Complete the sentences with the words in the list. There are two extra words.**

angry | exciting | expensive | fast | hungry | Japan
Japanese | old | Russian | terrible | thirsty | tired

1 Pianos aren't cheap. They're _____ .

2 Aki is from Japan. She's _____ .

3 Dmitri is from Moscow. He's _____ .

4 The car isn't _____ . It's very slow.

5 My phone is _____ . It isn't new.

6 Dad is _____ . He isn't happy.

7 It's very late. I'm _____ . Good night.

8 Water? Yes, please. I'm really _____ .

9 The new James Bond movie is really good. It's so _____ !

10 This restaurant is bad. The food is _____ .

GRAMMAR

4 **Complete the dialogues with the missing words.**

1 A Do ⁰ _you_ like ice cream?
    B Yes, I love ¹_____ .

2 A ²_____ you like dogs?
    B No, I don't like ³_____ .

3 A Do you like Lucy?
    B Yes, I like ⁴_____ . ⁵_____ is nice.

4 A Do you like Mr. Henderson?
    B No, I don't like ⁶_____ . ⁷_____ 's boring.

5 **Complete the sentences with the correct form of *be*. Use contracted forms.**

0 I _'m not_ (✗) Spanish. I _'m_ Portuguese.

1 I _____ (✗) 10 years old. I _____ 11.

2 A _____ David happy?
    B No, he _____ .

3 Henry and Sally _____ from Australia.

4 A _____ you hungry?
    B Yes, we _____ .

5 Maria _____ (✗) 12. She _____ 11.

6 A Why _____ you angry?
    B Because you _____ late.

7 A How old _____ they?
    B Kevin _____ 5 and Sally _____ 8.

8 A Where _____ Ella from?
    B She _____ from South Africa.

DIALOGUE

6 Put the dialogue in order

	NICKY	I'm great. It's my birthday today.
	NICKY	I know. I'm really excited.
	NICKY	Bye.
	NICKY	Thanks. I'm on my way to the new pizza restaurant.
1	NICKY	Hi, Simon, how's it going?
	SIMON	Well, have fun. See you later.
	SIMON	Awesome. Happy Birthday!
	SIMON	Oh, hi, Nicky. I'm fine. How about you?
	SIMON	The new pizza restaurant? It's great.

READING

7 Read the text and complete the information in the form.

Personal information

Name: 0 _Brad Armstrong_

Age: 1 _____

Nationality: 2 _____

Likes: 3 _____

Favorite sportsperson: 4 _____

Favorite singer: 5 _____

Best friend: 6 _____

My name is Brad Armstrong. I'm 13 years old.
I'm from the U.S. I live in Dallas.
I really like sports. I like basketball and soccer. My
favorite sportsperson is Tim Howard. He's a soccer
player. He's a goalkeeper and he's great.
I also like music. My favorite singer is Ed Sheeran. He's
a British singer. He's really good.
My best friend is Lisa. She's 13, too, and she's at my
school.

8 Read the text again and correct the sentences.

0 Brad is from the U.K.
  Brad is from the U.S.

1 Brad's home town is Chicago.
  _____

2 Brad really likes baseball.
  _____

3 Tim Howard is a tennis player.
  _____

4 Brad's favorite singer is a woman.
  _____

5 Brad's best friend is a boy.
  _____

6 Lisa is 12.
  _____

7 Lisa isn't at his school.
  _____

WRITING

9 Write a short text about you. Use the questions to help you. Write 35–50 words.

- What's your name?
- How old are you?
- Where you are from and what is your nationality?
- What things do you like?
- Who is your favorite sportsperson?
- Who is your favorite singer?
- Who is your best friend?

3 | ME AND MY FAMILY

GRAMMAR

Possessive 's SB page 32

1 ★★☆ Follow the lines and complete the sentences. Use 's.

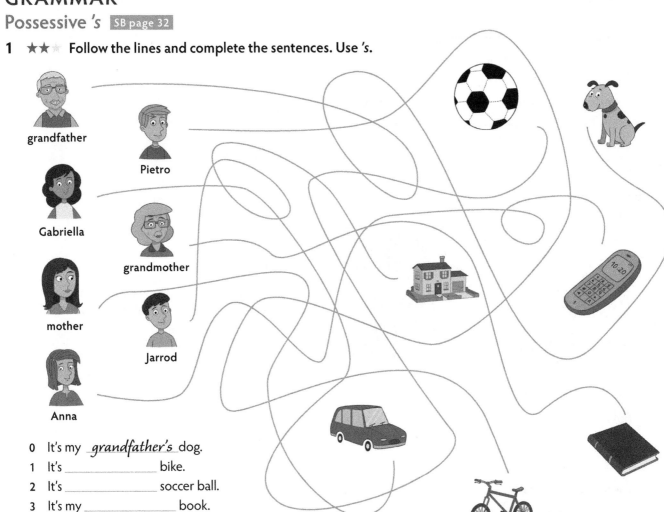

grandfather

Pietro

Gabriella

grandmother

mother

Jarrod

Anna

0 It's my _grandfather's_ dog.
1 It's _____ bike.
2 It's _____ soccer ball.
3 It's my _____ book.
4 It's my _____ car.
5 It's _____ house.
6 It's _____ phone.

Possessive adjectives SB page 33

2 ★☆☆ Complete the table.

	Possessive adjective
I	*my*
you	
he	
she	
we	
they	

3 ★★☆ Jake and Carly are at a birthday party. Circle the correct possessive adjectives.

JAKE Hi! What's ¹*your / his* name?

CARLY Carly.

JAKE Is that girl ²*her / your* friend?

CARLY Well, no. That's ³*my / their* sister. ⁴*His / Her* name's Maddie. This is ⁵*our / your* house.

JAKE Oh. And those two boys?

CARLY They're ⁶*your / my* brothers. They're twins. They're 12 today. It's ⁷*their / our* birthday party. Wait a minute. Who are you?

JAKE I'm Jake. I'm with Mark. I'm ⁸*her / his* cousin.

CARLY Well, welcome to the party!

4 ★★ Complete the sentences.

0 It's George's dog. It's ___*his*___ dog.
1 It's my mother's book. It's _____ book.
2 They're Jenny's books. They're _____ books.
3 It's Marin and Kate's apartment. It's _____ apartment.
4 It's my brother's and my TV. It's _____ TV.
5 They're John's CDs. They're _____ CDs.
6 It's my grandfather's chair. It's _____ chair.
7 I have three cousins – that's _____ house.
8 That's my family's car. It's _____ car.
9 A Is that _____ phone on the table?
   B No, this is _____ phone in my hand.
10 A Is _____ name Nina?
   B No, _____ name is Lara.

this / that / these / those SB page 34

5 ★★ (Circle) the correct answers (A, B, or C).

0 _____ is my bedroom.
   (A) This   B These   C Those
1 _____ is my new tablet.
   A Those   B That   C These
2 _____ are photos of my family.
   A That   B These   C This
3 _____ computer on the table is my sister's.
   A Those   B These   C That
4 Are _____ your books over there?
   A these   B that   C those
5 Is _____ a good movie?
   A these   B this   C those
6 _____ boys are from Brazil.
   A This   B That   C Those
7 _____ hotel is very expensive.
   A That   B Those   C These
8 _____ computer here is really slow.
   A That   B This   C These
9 Are _____ soccer players Brazilian?
   A this   B those   C that
10 Is _____ his pen?
   A these   B those   C this

6 ★★ Complete the sentences with *this*, *that*, *these*, or *those*.

0 ___*These*___ are the books I want, here.
1 _____ are my friends, over there.
2 _____ is my new phone, right here.
3 _____ are my new CDs, here.
4 _____ is my father, over there.
5 _____ is my bed, right here.
6 _____ are my cousins, there.
7 _____ is my brother's laptop, right there.
8 _____ are my DVDs, here.

GET IT RIGHT!

this and *these*

We use *this* to talk about singular objects that are near to us.
We use *these* to talk about plural objects that are near to us.

✓ **This** is my favorite dress.
✗ ~~These~~ is my favorite dress.
✓ **These** are my books.
✗ ~~This~~ are my books

Complete the sentences with *this* or *these*.

0 He gave me ___*this*___ shirt.
1 Is _____ your pencil?
2 _____ are my favorite shoes.
3 I got _____ book yesterday.
4 Are _____ your computer games?
5 _____ are my old sneakers.
6 I like _____ photo.
7 _____ cars are made in Japan, I think.
8 _____ car is really fast!

Pronunciation
this / that / these / those
Go to page 118.

VOCABULARY

Family members

MALE	FEMALE
son	daughter
father	mother
brother	sister
grandfather	grandmother
uncle	aunt
husband	wife
grandson	granddaughter
cousin	cousin

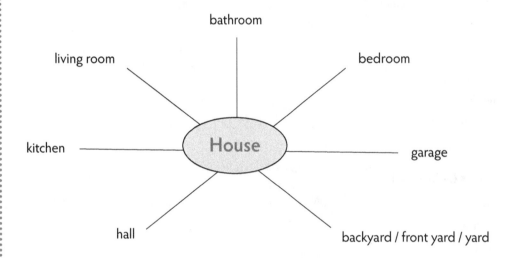

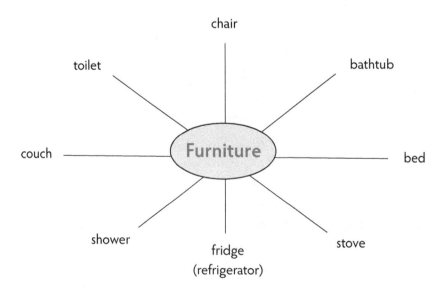

Key words in context

apartment	We live in an **apartment** on the 6th floor.
curtains	In my bedroom, there are green **curtains** on the window.
home	The house is very small, but it's my **home** and I love it.
photograph	I take great **photographs** with my new camera.
prince	He's the son of the king, so he's a **prince**.
queen	The U.K. and Denmark both have a **queen**.

Family members   SB page 32

1 ★☆☆ **Complete the words.**

0 au *n t*
1 _ o _
2 _ o _ _ e _
3 _ u _ a _ _
4 _ i _ e
5 _ o u _ i _
6 _ _ a _ _ o _ _ e _
7 _ _ a _ _ a _ e _
8 _ _ a _ _ o _

2 ★★☆ **Complete the puzzle. What's the mystery word?**

1		O							
	2			T					
	3			S					
	4				H				
5				E					
6				E					
	7			G					

1 My _____ is 45; she's a teacher.
2 My _____ Julie is my mother's sister.
3 My little _____ is only five years old.
4 I'm 12 and my _____ is 14.
5 My _____ is from London. He's English.
6 My _____ Paolo is from Brazil.
7 Our teacher's _____ is in our class.

3 ★★★ **Write answers to the questions so they are true for you.**

1 Is your family big or small?

_____

2 What are your parents' names?

_____

3 How many cousins do you have?

_____

4 How many aunts and uncles do you have?

_____

5 Where do the people in your family live?

_____

6 How many people do you live with?

_____

House and furniture   SB page 35

4 ★☆☆ (Circle) **the odd one out in each list.**

0	bathtub	shower	(couch)
1	chair	bedroom	kitchen
2	shower	hall	bathroom
3	stove	bed	fridge
4	bedroom	garage	living room
5	garage	kitchen	yard
6	toilet	hall	kitchen

5 ★★☆ **Look at photos 1–5. Where do you find these things in a house? Write the words.**

0 *living room*

1 _____

2 _____

3 _____

4 _____

5 _____

6 ★★★ **Are these things in the correct place? Mark ✓ (yes, OK), ? (maybe), or ✗ (no).**

1 a shower in the backyard ☐
2 a couch in the bedroom ☐
3 a car in the garage ☐
4 a fridge in the bedroom ☐
5 a stove in the garage ☐
6 a car in the hall ☐
7 a toilet in the bathroom ☐
8 a chair in the yard ☐

READING

1 **REMEMBER AND CHECK** **Mark the sentences T (true) or F (false). Then look at the article on page 31 of the Student's Book and check your answers.**

0 Kate Middleton is English.   `T`

1 She likes playing soccer.   ☐

2 Kate's family is from Scotland.   ☐

3 She has a sister named Elizabeth.   ☐

4 Kate is very famous now.   ☐

5 William's grandfather is Prince Charles.   ☐

6 She has a daughter named Ann.   ☐

7 Kate's home is a small house.   ☐

2 **Read the blog quickly. Is Marnie's family big or small?**

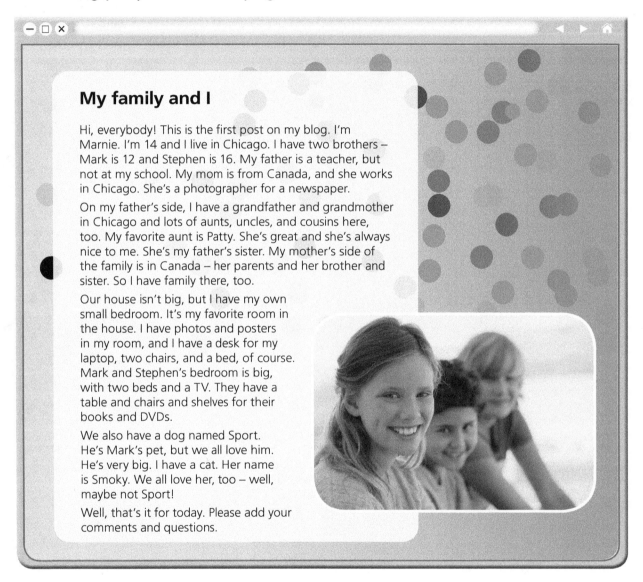

My family and I

Hi, everybody! This is the first post on my blog. I'm Marnie. I'm 14 and I live in Chicago. I have two brothers – Mark is 12 and Stephen is 16. My father is a teacher, but not at my school. My mom is from Canada, and she works in Chicago. She's a photographer for a newspaper.

On my father's side, I have a grandfather and grandmother in Chicago and lots of aunts, uncles, and cousins here, too. My favorite aunt is Patty. She's great and she's always nice to me. She's my father's sister. My mother's side of the family is in Canada – her parents and her brother and sister. So I have family there, too.

Our house isn't big, but I have my own small bedroom. It's my favorite room in the house. I have photos and posters in my room, and I have a desk for my laptop, two chairs, and a bed, of course. Mark and Stephen's bedroom is big, with two beds and a TV. They have a table and chairs and shelves for their books and DVDs.

We also have a dog named Sport. He's Mark's pet, but we all love him. He's very big. I have a cat. Her name is Smoky. We all love her, too – well, maybe not Sport!

Well, that's it for today. Please add your comments and questions.

3 **Read the blog again and complete the sentences with words from the text.**

0 Marnie has two ___*brothers*___ , Mark and Stephen.

1 Her father is a _____ .

2 Her mother is from _____ .

3 Her mother is a _____ .

4 Marnie has family in _____ and in _____ .

5 Marnie's favorite aunt is named _____ .

6 Marnie's favorite room is her _____ .

7 Her brothers have two _____ and a TV in their room.

DEVELOPING WRITING

My bedroom

1 Read the text. Find three or more differences between Jake's perfect bedroom and his real bedroom.

> **My perfect bedroom and my real bedroom**
>
> My perfect bedroom is big. The walls are yellow, and the floor is brown. The bed is very big – it's 2 meters long and 1.6 meters wide (I like big beds!). It's very comfortable, too, and it's the color of my favorite soccer team. So it's black and white because my favorite team is Juventus. The desk is near the window, with a comfortable chair for me to sit and work on my great new computer.
>
> My real bedroom isn't big. The floor is brown but the walls are blue. The bed is OK, but it isn't very big and it isn't very comfortable! The bed is black and white – yay! My desk is near the door and the chair is small but it's OK. And I like my computer. It's old but it's really good!

2 Complete the sentences with *and* or *but*.

0 The walls are yellow, _____ *and* _____ the floor is brown.

1 The bed is big, _____ it's comfortable.

2 The bed is comfortable, _____ it's in Juventus colors, too.

3 The computer is old, _____ it's really good.

3 Think about your perfect bedroom and about your real bedroom. Use the ideas below to help you make notes.

	My real bedroom	My perfect bedroom
big / small?		
wall color?		
floor color?		
big / small bed?		
comfortable?		
bed color?		
near the window?		
chair?		

4 Use your notes to write about your real bedroom and your perfect bedroom.

My real bedroom

My real bedroom _____ big. The floor is _____ , and the walls are _____ . The bed is _____ . The bed is _____ . The _____ is near the window. The chair is _____ .

My perfect bedroom

My perfect bedroom _____ big. The floor is _____ , and the walls are _____ . The bed is _____ . The bed is _____ . The _____ is near the window. The chair is _____ .

LISTENING

1 🔊18 **Listen to the dialogue and complete the sentences. Write *Tony*, *Christine*, or *Jack*.**

0 *Christine* says the room is nice.

1 _____ is Tony's brother.

2 _____ likes watching soccer.

3 _____ loves movies.

4 The CDs are _____ 's.

2 🔊18 **Listen again and complete the words in this part of the dialogue.**

CHRISTINE   Wow! Are these your DVDs, Tony?
They're ⁰g *reat*_____ !
I ¹l_____ movies.

TONY   No, they're my brother's. He really
²l_____ old movies. Very, very old
movies.

CHRISTINE   ³W_____ a ⁴n_____
collection!

TONY   Yeah. It's not bad. But the movies are a little
boring!

CHRISTINE   No, they're great! Hey! Are these your CDs?
They're ⁵f_____ ! This one
⁶l_____ really ⁷c_____ !

TONY   Yeah, I ⁸r_____ ⁹l_____ Ella
Henderson. She's my favorite. She's a great
singer.

CHRISTINE   Let's listen to it now!

TONY   OK.

DIALOGUE

1 **Put the dialogues in order.**

Dialogue 1

☐	LUCY	Yes, it is cool. I love T-shirts!
1	LUCY	Happy birthday, Pat! This is a present for you.
☐	LUCY	This one? It's from Italy. It's a birthday present from my Italian friend.
☐	PAT	For me? Thanks, Lucy! Oh, a T-shirt! And it's really cool!
☐	PAT	Your T-shirt's nice, too. I really like it.

Dialogue 2

☐	JIM	Thank you! Come into the kitchen. My mom and dad are there.
1	JIM	Hi, Ally! Nice to see you. Come in!
☐	JIM	No, he isn't. He's in his bedroom.
☐	ALLY	Is your brother there, too?
☐	ALLY	Hi, Jim. Thanks. Wow, I really like your house.

2 **Look at Exercise 1 and complete the dialogues between you and a friend.**

Dialogue 1

YOU   I really ¹*like / love* your shirt. Is it new?

FRIEND   Yes, it's from ²_____ .

YOU   It looks ³*great / nice / fantastic*.

FRIEND   Thanks.

Dialogue 2

YOU   What a ⁴*nice / great / fantastic* CD!

FRIEND   Yes, it's by ⁵_____ .

YOU   I really ⁶*like / love* it.

FRIEND   Let's listen to it now.

Dialogue 3

YOU   What a ⁷*fantastic / good / great* computer game!

FRIEND   Yes. It's called ⁸_____ .

YOU   I really ⁹*love / like* computer games.

FRIEND   OK. Let's play it together!

3 **Now write your own dialogue.**

PHRASES FOR FLUENCY

SB page 37

1 ★ ☆ ☆ **Complete the phrases with the missing vowels.**

0 R e a lly?

1 _h, r_ght.

2 L_ t's g_.

3 J_st _ m_n_t_.

2 **Complete the dialogue with the phrases in the list.**

just a minute | let's go | oh, right | ~~really~~

ANA   That boy over there is really cool.

JO   ⁰_____*Really*_____ ? Him? Well, he isn't my favorite person.

ANA   I think he's cool.

JO   Well, he is, but sometimes he's difficult.

ANA   Hey, ¹_____ . Isn't he in your family?

JO   Yeah, he's my brother.

ANA   ²_____ . Your brother. OK.

JO   Ana, ³_____ ! We're late for class!

Sum it up

1 Look at the pictures and complete the crossword.

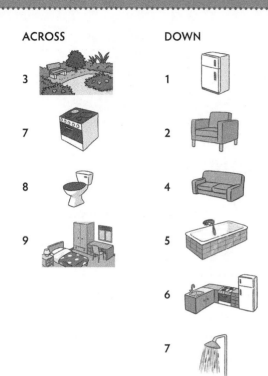

ACROSS

DOWN

2 Read the website about a famous house. Which of the things in the house is impossible to have?

Upton Manor

⦿⦿⦿⦿◯

Come and visit Upton Manor! This famous house is 400 years old. The Hogworth family lives here – Lord Hogworth, Lady Hogworth, and their four children.

Walk in the big front yard! Take a tour of the house and see its 20 bedrooms! Look at the wonderful 400-year-old kitchen with its 300-year-old fridge!

See 10 fantastic old cars in the garage. See the old bathtubs in the bathrooms. Everything here is old and interesting!

Open weekends, 10 a.m. to 5 p.m. Only $10.00 per person or $25.00 for a family.

3 Complete the page from the website with information from the text.

- 0Age of house   *400 years old*
- 1Owners' family name _____
- 2Number of bedrooms _____
- 3Age of kitchen _____
- 4Number of cars _____
- 5Opening time _____
- 6Closing time _____
- 7Days open every week _____
- 8Price per person _____
- 9Price for a family _____

4 IN THE CITY

GRAMMAR

there is / there are SB page 40

1 ★☆☆ **Complete the sentences with *is* or *are*.**

0 There _____are_____ four bedrooms in the house.

1 There _____ two Brazilian girls at our school.

2 There _____ lots of famous buildings in Paris.

3 There _____ a mountain near Tokyo called Mount Fuji.

4 _____ there a desk in your bedroom?

5 There _____ a small couch in my parents' bedroom.

6 There _____ two or three train stations in my city.

7 There _____ eight people in my family.

8 _____ there any good stores near here?

2 ★★☆ **Complete the text with *there is*, *there isn't*, *there are*, or *there aren't*.**

> Alice is 14. Here is what she says about *Rosewood*, her local mall.
>
> "I really like our local mall. It's small, but ⁰ *there is* a movie theater. ¹_____ some cafés on the top floor, but ²_____ any restaurants. My mom likes it because ³_____ two good bookstores and ⁴_____ a great hair salon. My sister likes it because ⁵_____ some cool clothing stores. My brother doesn't like it because ⁶_____ a good sporting goods store (and he loves sports!). My dad doesn't like the mall. He says ⁷_____ too many people there."

some / any SB page 40

3 ★☆☆ **Circle the correct options.**

0 There are (some) / any books in my room.

1 There aren't *some* / *any* good stores here.

2 There are *some* / *any* nice clothes in that store.

3 There aren't *some* / *any* good books in the school library.

4 There aren't *some* / *any* banks on this street.

5 There are *some* / *any* interesting things in the museum.

6 There aren't *some* / *any* cafés in the park.

7 There are *some* / *any* supermarkets in the town center.

8 There are *some* / *any* chairs in the yard.

4 ★★☆ **Complete the sentences with *some* or *any*.**

0 There are _____some_____ good stores.

1 There aren't _____ sporting goods stores.

2 There aren't _____ movie theaters.

3 There are _____ computer stores.

4 There aren't _____ phone stores.

5 There are _____ cafés.

5 ★★☆ **Complete the text with *there is a*, *there isn't a*, *there are some*, or *there aren't any*.**

> Tim is 12. This is what he thinks of *Parkland*, his local mall.
>
> "The mall near my house is really big. There are about 400 stores. I like Parkland because ⁰ *there are some* good clothing stores and a movie theater, too. Mom says ¹_____ good shoe stores, but they're not my favorite places. ²_____ DVD store and ³_____ great skateboard shops. The only bad thing is that ⁴_____ computer stores and ⁵_____ nice restaurants – just fast food places. But ⁶_____ interesting cooking store, and ⁷_____ little ice cream shop with great Italian ice cream."

6 ★★★ Complete the questions with *Is there a* or *Are there any.* Then look at the texts in Exercises 2 and 5 and answer the questions. Use *Yes, there is/are.*, *No, there isn't/aren't.*, or *I don't know.*

0 *Is there a* _____ hair salon at *Rosewood?*
   Yes, there is. _____

1 _____ movie theaters in *Rosewood?*
   _____

2 _____ computer stores at *Rosewood?*
   _____

3 _____ clothing stores at *Rosewood?*
   _____

4 _____ sporting goods stores
   at *Rosewood?*
   _____

5 _____ bank at *Parkland?*
   _____

6 _____ nice restaurant at *Parkland?*
   _____

7 _____ movie theater at *Parkland?*
   _____

8 _____ music stores at *Parkland?*
   _____

9 _____ place to get ice cream
   at *Parkland?*
   _____

7 ★★★ Complete these sentences about a mall you know.

1 There are _____ .
2 There aren't _____ .
3 There aren't _____ .
4 There are _____ .
5 There is _____ .
6 There isn't _____ .

Imperatives SB page 41

8 ★☆☆ Circle the correct options.

0 OK, everyone. Please *listen* / *don't listen* to me. This is important.
1 Are you tired? *Go* / *Don't go* to bed late tonight.
2 Please *be* / *don't be* quiet in the library.
3 It's cold in here. *Open* / *Don't open* the window, please.
4 Hello. Please come in and *sit* / *don't sit* down.
5 Wow! *Look* / *Don't look* at that fantastic statue.
6 It's a very expensive store! *Buy* / *Don't buy* your new clothes there!
7 To get to the movie theater, *turn* / *don't turn* left at the supermarket, and it's there.
8 *Listen* / *Don't listen* to your brother. He's wrong.

9 ★★☆ Mick and Josh are looking for a sporting goods store. Complete the dialogue with the words in the list.

go | listen to | look | open | sit down | turn

MICK Where's the sporting goods store?
JOSH OK, 0 *sit down* on this chair and
      1_____ at the map.
MICK I don't have a map.
JOSH Oh, well, I have an app.
MICK Well 2_____ the app on your phone, then.
JOSH OK, OK. Wait a minute. Oh! Look, there's the sporting goods store. 3_____ down here and 4_____ left. It's behind the drugstore.
MICK Is it across from the phone store?
JOSH No, 5_____ me! It's on the corner, behind the drugstore.

GET IT RIGHT! ◉

some and *any*

We use *some* in affirmative sentences and *any* in negative sentences.

✓ I have **some** time.
✗ I have ~~any~~ time.
✓ He doesn't have **any** money.
✗ He doesn't have ~~some~~ money.

Complete the sentences with *some* or *any.*

0 I don't have ____*any*____ pets.
1 There are _____ good games on TV today.
2 Don't bring _____ food.
3 They don't have _____ homework.
4 I have _____ time to help you this afternoon.
5 I have _____ presents for you.
6 We don't have _____ problems with our neighbors.

VOCABULARY

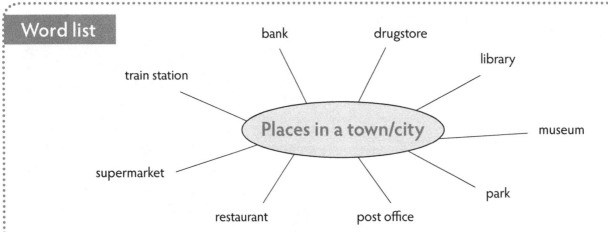

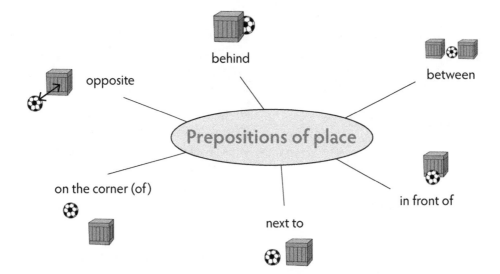

Numbers 100+

one hundred (and) thirty	130
one hundred (and) fifty	150
one hundred (and) seventy-five	175
two hundred	200
five hundred (and) sixty	560
one thousand	1,000
one thousand two hundred	1,200
two thousand	2,000

Prices

dollar	$
pound	£
euro	€
nine dollars and ninety-nine cents	$9.99
twenty-one ninety-five	$21.95
seventy-two euros fifty	€72.50

Key words in context

bookstore	This is a great **bookstore**. They have books in different languages here.
expensive	That shirt is $150.00. It's very **expensive**!
famous	The Eiffel Tower in Paris is very **famous**.
palace	The king and queen live in that **palace**. It has 20 bedrooms!
shoe store	There's a new **shoe store** in town. Their shoes are really nice!
square	The **square** in front of St. Peter's Basilica in Rome is very big.
statue	There's a nice **statue** of the queen in the museum.
tower	The CN **Tower** in Toronto is 553 meters tall!

Places in a town/city SB page 40

1 ★★★ **Where are these people? Write a word from the list.**

bank | drugstore | library | museum
park | ~~post office~~ | restaurant
supermarket | train station

0 Hi. Can I send this letter to Australia, please?
_____*post office*_____

1 Six apples and some bananas, please.
_____

2 Look! These things are 200 years old!
_____

3 A round-trip ticket to Boston, please.
_____

4 Please be quiet in here. People are reading.
_____

5 It's a great day for a picnic here.
_____

6 Hi. Can I change these dollars into pounds, please?
_____

7 The steak and salad for me, please.
_____

8 I need some medicine for my eye.
_____

Prepositions of place SB page 41

2 ★★★ **Look at the map of the mall and (circle) the correct options.**

0 The computer store is *behind* / *next to* the bank.
1 The computer store is *between* / *in front of* the bank and the bookstore.
2 The bookstore is *across from* / *on the corner*.
3 The shoe store is *between* / *across from* the supermarket.
4 The bank is *next to* / *behind* the shoe store.
5 The café is *behind* / *in front of* the movie theater.

Pronunciation

Word stress in numbers
Go to page 119.

3 ★★★ **Use the prepositions in Exercise 2 to complete the sentences.**

0 The drugstore is ___*next to*___ the supermarket.
1 The restaurant is _____ the shoe store.
2 The post office is _____ the restaurant and the phone store.
3 The restaurant is _____ the supermarket.
4 The sporting goods store is _____ the drugstore.
5 The movie theater is _____ the café.
6 The phone store is _____ the bookstore.

Numbers 100+ SB page 42

4 ★★★ **Write the words or numbers.**

0	110	*one hundred and ten*
1	_____	one hundred and seventeen
2	125	
3	_____	one hundred and ninety-eight
4	215	
5	_____	three hundred and twelve
6	652	
7	_____	one thousand three hundred
8	1,400	
9	_____	two thousand six hundred and twenty

Prices SB page 43

5 ★★★ **Write the prices in words.**

$12.50

£ 65.50

0 *twelve dollars and fifty cents*

1 _____

€ 120.00

£ 275.95

2 _____

3 _____

$145.00

€ 1,600.00

4 _____

5 _____

6 ★★★ **Write the name of something you know.**

1 a famous tower _____
2 a good museum _____
3 a beautiful square _____
4 an interesting palace _____

READING

1 REMEMBER AND CHECK (Circle) the correct options. Then look at the brochure on page 39 of the Student's Book and check your answers.

0 Shenzhen is a (city) / river.

1 Window of the World is in *China* / *Japan*.

2 It's a *museum* / *park*.

3 There are models of famous places from around *China* / *the world*.

4 You can take a ride on the *Hudson* / *Colorado* River.

5 China's national day is *January 1* / *October 1*.

6 There is a festival of *Chinese* / *pop* music every year.

7 There *are some* / *aren't any* restaurants in the park.

2 Read the emails quickly. Who lives in Australia?

From: Jack
To: HarryP@mail.com
Subject: New home

Hi, Harry!

How are things in Sydney? Is it warm and sunny there? It's winter vacation now, and it's very cold and wet here in Canada. That's nothing new! December isn't my favorite month. There's some soccer on TV, but there are a lot of shows about cooking and people dancing. There's a new café in town, but it's between a museum and the library. There are always a lot of old ladies in it – no young people.

I'm bored! Please email and tell me about Australia.

Jack

From: Harry
To: JackM@mail.com
Subject: Re: New home

Hi, Jack!

Thanks for your email. I love it here. It's vacation time here, too, but we're still in Sydney. And yes, it's very hot and sunny. There are some great beaches and lots of things to do. Our apartment isn't in the center of town; it's across from the beach! Sydney is fantastic. There are great movie theaters and museums, parks and, of course, Sydney Harbour Bridge and the famous Opera House. The bridge is beautiful, but opera isn't my favorite music. There are lots of great places to eat and some really cool cafés. My mom loves all the malls.

Next email, all about my new school!!!!

Harry

3 Read the emails again. Mark the sentences T (true) or F (false).

0 It's December. `T`

1 Harry and Jack are on vacation. ☐

2 There's a new shoe store in Jack's town. ☐

3 Jack loves the new café. ☐

4 Harry lives in a house. ☐

5 There are lots of movie theaters in Sydney. ☐

6 Harry's favorite music is opera. ☐

7 Harry's mom likes the malls. ☐

8 Harry is at a new school. ☐

DEVELOPING WRITING

Your city

1 Read the text. Does the writer like weekends in her city?

A weekend in my city

I like my city. It isn't very big, but the people here are nice.

On the weekend, there are a lot of things to do. The downtown is small, but there are some great stores and cafés, so I always go downtown on Saturday mornings to meet my friends. We have something to eat together, or we do some shopping. Some days we don't buy anything, but it's always fun.

There's a movie theater in the city, too, so on Saturday nights or Sunday afternoons, my friends and I see a movie together. I like baseball, so on Sunday mornings I play with lots of friends in the park. It's really fun.

Not far from downtown there is a river. It's great to swim there, but only in the summer!

My city is OK and my friends are great, so the weekends here aren't bad.

2 Complete the sentences with *or*, *and*, or *so*.

1 On Saturday evenings we go to the movie theater _____ watch a movie.

2 Do you want to play baseball _____ volleyball?

3 My cousins live 300 kilometers away, _____ I don't visit them very often.

3 Match the words with the phrases.

1 in ☐

2 on ☐

a the weekend

b the summer

4 Think about weekends in your city. What do you do? Use these ideas to help you make notes.

What I do on Saturday _____

_____

What I do on Sunday _____

_____

What I do with my friends _____

_____

What we do in the summer _____

_____

What we do in the winter _____

_____

5 Use your notes to complete the text.

Weekends in my city

I live in _____ . I _____ my city.
_____ the weekend, I _____ Saturday mornings.
_____ Saturday afternoons I _____ . Sundays
I _____ . With my friends I _____ .
_____ the summer we _____ , but _____
the winter we _____ .

LISTENING

1 🔊20 **Listen to Stella and Matt talking to their Aunt Louisa. Check (✓) the places they talk about.**

bank	☐
bookstore	☐
café	☐
drugstore	☐
library	☐
museum	✓
park	☐
post office	☐
mall	☐
station	☐
supermarket	☐

2 🔊20 **Listen again and correct the sentences.**

0 There isn't a good mall.
   There's a good mall.

1 The museum is on Grand Boulevard.
   _____

2 The museum is very big.
   _____

3 The mall is next to the museum.
   _____

4 Stella wants some pens and pencils for her project.
   _____

5 There aren't any places to eat in the mall.
   _____

6 Aunt Louisa's favorite café is next to the bookstore.
   _____

DIALOGUE

1 **Stella is in a clothing store. Put the dialogue in order.**

☐	WOMAN	$15.50.
☐	WOMAN	OK. That's $31.00, please.
1	WOMAN	Hello. Can I help you?
☐	WOMAN	Yes. There's this one here.
☐	STELLA	Hi. Yes. Do you have any yellow T-shirts?
☐	STELLA	Great! I'll take two, please.
☐	STELLA	Oh, it's really nice. How much is it?

2 **Complete the dialogue with the words and phrases in the list.**

~~Can~~ | expensive | is | much | That's | three

MAN   ⁰ __*Can*__ I help you?

MATTHEW   Yes, do you have any maps of the town?

MAN   Yes, there are ¹_____ different maps.

MATTHEW   How ²_____ are they?

MAN   They're $1.50 each.

MATTHEW   OK, all three, please.

MAN   That's $4.50.

MATTHEW   And how much ³_____ that small book about the museum?

MAN   It's $5.70.

MATTHEW   And that big book?

MAN   That's $25.00.

MATTHEW   That's very ⁴_____. Just the maps and the small book, please.

MAN   OK. ⁵_____ $10.20, please.

3 **Imagine you're in a bookstore. Write a dialogue similar to the ones above.**

_____
_____
_____
_____
_____
_____
_____
_____

▮▮ TRAIN TO THINK ▮▮

Exploring numbers

Seth and John have to buy things for their room at home. They have $300. They buy five things and they have $35 left. Check (✓) what they buy.

couch – $60	☐
bed – $50	☐
chair – $20	☐
desk – $30	☐
speakers for their music players – $25	☐
table – $35	☐
TV – $100	☐

EXAM SKILLS: Listening

Identifying text type

1 🔊21 Listen to people talking in three different situations. How many people are speaking?

Situation 1: _____

Situation 2: _____

Situation 3: _____

2 Match the descriptions with the pictures. Write 1–3 in the boxes.

1 a news report on TV

2 an announcement at a train station

3 people in a store

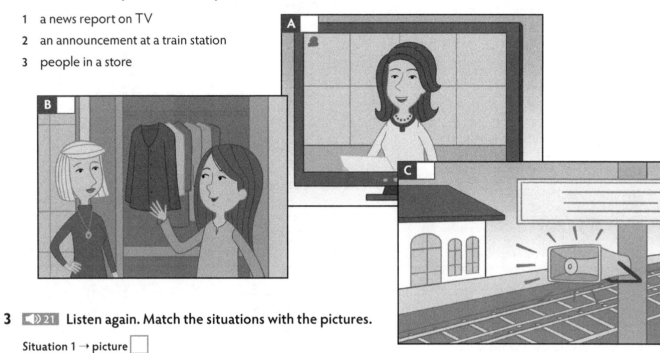

3 🔊21 Listen again. Match the situations with the pictures.

Situation 1 → picture ☐

Situation 2 → picture ☐

Situation 3 → picture ☐

Listening tip

When you listen to a text for the first time, you don't need to understand every word.
Listen to the important things:

● Number of speakers.

● Sounds and noises to tell you where the speakers are.

● The way the speakers talk, are they happy, angry, worried, sad, excited, bored?

● "Important" words – read the question first and think of words (nouns, adjectives, or verbs) that might help you to answer it. These are "important" words to listen for.

---

4 🔊21 Listen again to the three situations. Which words helped you in Exercise 3?

Situation 1: _____

Situation 2: _____

Situation 3: _____

CONSOLIDATION

LISTENING

1 🔊22 **Listen to Jeff talking about his family and where they live. (Circle) the correct answers (A, B, or C).**

1 How many people are there in Jeff's family?

A six   B eight   C ten

2 How many sisters does Jeff have?

A four   B five   C six

3 Where is Jeff from?

A the U.S.   B the U.K.   C Canada

4 What's his cousin's name?

A Kate   B Brad   C Billy

2 🔊22 **Listen again. How many are there? Write the numbers in the boxes.**

VOCABULARY

3 **Match the words in A with the words in B to make pairs.**

A

bathroom	uncle
living room	brother
son	kitchen
garage	husband

B

car	daughter
couch	stove
wife	sister
shower	aunt

0 _bathroom — shower_

1 _____

2 _____

3 _____

4 _____

5 _____

6 _____

7 _____

4 **Name the stores and write the prices.**

○ $3.29

0   _drugstore — It's three twenty-nine._

○ $14.99

1 _____

○ £2.50

2 _____

○ €79.59

3 _____

○ $12.99

4 _____

GRAMMAR

5 **Complete the sentences with the words in the list. There are two extra words.**

any | her | his | is | some | their | those | turn

1 Ask Luke. It's _____ sandwich.
2 There _____ a big park near my house.
3 Paul is Danny and Olivia's brother. He's _____ brother.
4 The shoe store? OK, just _____ right on High Street and it's there.
5 There aren't _____ parks near here.
6 Can I see _____ T-shirts in the window, please?

DIALOGUE

6 **Complete the dialogue.**

JORDAN   I like your T-shirt, Rachel.
RACHEL   ¹R _____ ? It's very old.
JORDAN   Well, I think it ²l_____ cool. And ³w_____ a great hat, too.
RACHEL   ⁴T_____ you. It's new.
JORDAN   How ⁵m_____ was it?
RACHEL   Well, it was a gift from my mom.
JORDAN   Oh, ⁶r_____ . I'll ask her then.

READING

7 **Read the dialogue and complete the sentences.**

WOMAN	Hello, can I help you?
JEFF	Yes, I'd like to see those T-shirts behind you.
WOMAN	These red ones?
JEFF	No, the blue ones next to them.
WOMAN	OK. Yes, these are really nice. Here you are.
JEFF	How much are they?
WOMAN	Wait a minute. Let me see. They're $9.99.
JEFF	OK, can I have three, please?
WOMAN	Wow. You really like them.
JEFF	They're not for me. They're for my sisters.
WOMAN	Your sisters?
JEFF	Yes. It's their birthday tomorrow.
WOMAN	So they're triplets?
JEFF	Yes, all three born on the same day.
WOMAN	Is it difficult? I mean having three sisters?
JEFF	Three! There are two more as well.
WOMAN	Five sisters! You poor thing. Here, have another T-shirt for you.
JEFF	Wow, thanks. That's really nice of you.

1 Jeff wants to see the _____ T-shirts.
2 The T-shirts are _____ each.
3 The T-shirts are for his _____ .
4 It's their _____ tomorrow.
5 Triplets are _____ children born on the same day.
6 Jeff has _____ sisters.
7 The woman gives Jeff a free _____ .
8 Jeff thinks the woman is very _____ .

WRITING

8 **Write a short text about your family and where you live. Write 35–50 words. Use the questions to help you.**

- Who is in your family?
- What is your house like?
- What is your city like?

5 IN MY FREE TIME

GRAMMAR

Simple present `SB page 50`

1 ★☆☆ (Circle) the correct options.

0 I (play)/ plays tennis every day.

1 My brothers *speak* / *speaks* Spanish.

2 Mr. Jones *teach* / *teaches* math.

3 The dog *like* / *likes* the park.

4 We sometimes *go* / *goes* to bed very late.

5 You *live* / *lives* near me.

2 ★★☆ Complete the sentences with the simple present form of the verbs in parentheses. Which four sentences match with the pictures? Write the numbers in the boxes.

0 My dad _____*flies*_____ planes. (fly)

1 The boys _____ a lot of video games. (play)

2 Ms. Dawes _____ English. (teach)

3 Suzanna _____ in the library every day. (study)

4 Tim and Dana _____ the guitar. (play)

5 Mom _____ flowers. (love)

A

B

C

D

3 ★★☆ Complete the sentences with the correct form of the verbs in the list.

finish | go | like | play | speak | study | teach | watch

0 Mom _____*likes*_____ pop music.

1 My father _____ music at my school.

2 Lucy _____ to a glee club on Wednesdays.

3 Sam _____ four languages. He's amazing.

4 My brother _____ TV on Saturday mornings.

5 Our school _____ at 3:15 p.m.

6 Jeff _____ the piano in the school band.

7 My aunt _____ at a school in Atlanta.

> ### Pronunciation
> Simple present verbs: third person
> **Go to page 119.** 🔊

Adverbs of frequency `SB page 50`

4 ★☆☆ Put the adverbs in the correct order.

☐ often   [1] always   ☐ sometimes   ☐ never

5 ★★☆ Write the sentences with the adverb of frequency in the correct place.

0 I meet my friends downtown on Saturdays. (often)
   I often meet my friends in town on Saturdays.

1 Kelly is happy. (always)
   _____

2 They do homework on the weekend. (never)
   _____

3 You help Dad make dinner. (sometimes)
   _____

4 We are tired on Friday afternoons. (often)
   _____

5 It rains on Saturdays! (always)
   _____

6 Mom flies to New York for work. (often)
   _____

7 I am bored in English classes. (never)
   _____

6 ★★★ Write sentences so they are true for you. Use adverbs of frequency.

1 do homework after school

_____

2 play sports on the weekend

_____

3 watch TV on Sunday mornings

_____

4 listen to music in the morning

_____

5 call my best friend in the evening

_____

Simple present (negative) SB page 51

7 ★★ Complete the sentences with the negative form of the verbs in parentheses.

0 My mom _____*doesn't write*_____ books for children. (write)

1 I _____ to soccer practice after school. (go)

2 My cousins _____ to a lot of music. (listen)

3 My dad _____ model planes. (make)

4 We _____ games on our tablet. (play)

5 School _____ at 8:15 a.m. (start)

6 My sister _____ singing or dancing. (like)

8 ★★ Match these sentences with the sentences in Exercise 7.

0	0	She writes for teenagers.
a		But the gates open at that time.
b		We play them on the computer.
c		She's very shy.
d		I go on Saturdays.
e		He makes trains.
f		But they watch a lot of TV.

Simple present (questions) SB page 52

9 ★ Complete the questions with *do* or *does*.

0 ___*Do*___ you live in Miami?

1 _____ Paul like sports?

2 _____ you know the answer?

3 _____ your sister play the piano?

4 _____ you often go to the movies?

5 _____ your teacher give you a lot of homework?

10 Write the questions. Then write answers to the questions so they are true for you.

0 your mother / speak English?
   Does your mother speak English?
   Yes, she does. / No, she doesn't.

1 you / always do your homework?

_____

_____

2 your best friend / play tennis?

_____

3 you / sometimes play computer games before school?

_____

_____

4 you and your friends / play soccer?

_____

_____

5 your mom / drive a car?

_____

_____

GET IT RIGHT! ◉
Adverbs of frequency

With the verb *be*, we use this word order: subject + verb + adverb of frequency.

With other verbs, we use this word order: subject + adverb of frequency + verb.

✓ *He is always friendly.*
✗ ~~He always is friendly.~~
✓ *I often watch football on TV.*
✗ ~~I watch often football on TV.~~

Circle the correct sentences.

0 a I eat often pizza.
  (b) I often eat pizza.

1 a I go out often with friends.
  b I often go out with friends.

2 a I always go to the movies with my friends.
  b Always I go to the movies with my friends.

3 a Their music is always great.
  b Their music always is great.

4 a I play soccer in the park never.
  b I never play soccer in the park.

5 a I sometimes am bored.
  b I am sometimes bored.

6 a Lucy often is late for school.
  b Lucy is often late for school.

VOCABULARY

Free-time activities

| play computer games | dance | hang out with friends | go shopping | do homework | chat with friends online |

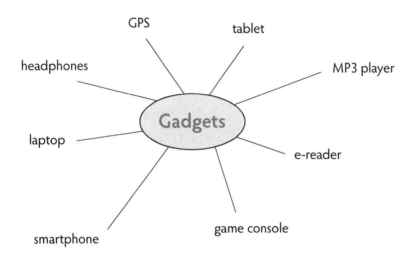

GPS   tablet

headphones   MP3 player

laptop   **Gadgets**   e-reader

smartphone   game console

Days of the week

MONDAY	TUESDAY	WEDNESDAY	THURSDAY	FRIDAY	SATURDAY	SUNDAY

Key words in context

carry	Don't **carry** all those books. They're very heavy.	**help**	Dad often **helps** me with my homework.
cheer	I always **cheer** when my team scores a goal.	**meet**	I sometimes **meet** my friends in the park on weekends.
concert	I often go to **concerts** at the stadium.	**perform**	My school **performs** a play every year.
end	School **ends** at 4 p.m.	**sing**	My dad always **sings** in the shower.
feel	I **feel** tired. I want to go to bed.	**study**	I **study** best in the late afternoon.
finish	I want to **finish** my book this weekend.	**teach**	Mr. Carlson **teaches** math.
fly	My mom **flies** planes for United Airlines.		

Free-time activities `SB page 50`

1 ★☆☆ **Match the parts of the sentences.**

0 I play — `e`
1 I go
2 I hang out with
3 I do
4 I listen to
5 I dance

a shopping with Dad on Saturdays.
b my homework when I get home.
c music in my bed.
d to rap music in my bedroom.
e computer games on my tablet.
f my friends in the park on Sundays.

2 ★★☆ **Complete the sentences with the words in the list.**

dance | his homework | listens
out | plays | shopping

0 Every day after school I hang ___*out*___ in the park.
1 Lisa goes _____ with her sister on Saturday mornings.
2 Tomas never does _____ on time.
3 In the movie, they _____ the tango with each other.
4 My brother _____ computer games all weekend!
5 My dad _____ to really old music!

3 ★★★ **Write sentences that are true for you. Use adverbs of frequency.**

1 play computer games
2 go shopping
3 dance
4 do homework
5 listen to music
6 hang out with friends
7 play sports
8 go to the movies

Gadgets `SB page 53`

4 ★★☆ **Unscramble the letters to make words for gadgets.**

0 blteat — *tablet*
1 mega loscone
2 P3M replay
3 marsthopen
4 ahehndspoe
5 SGP
6 plapto
7 arae-der

5 ★★★ **Answer the questions so they are true for you.**

1 Q What do you use to play computer games?
   A _____
2 Q What do you use to listen to music?
   A _____
3 Q What do you use to find your way?
   A _____
4 Q What do you use to read books, magazines, or articles?
   A _____

Days of the week `SB page 53`

6 ★★☆ **Complete the days of the week with the missing letters. Then put the days in order.**

`1` M _o_ nday
☐ ___ dnesday
☐ ___ iday
☐ ___ esday
☐ ___ nday
☐ ___ ursday
☐ ___ turday

7 ★★★ **Choose three days. Write sentences so they are true for you.**

I love Fridays because I always go to the movies with my dad in the evening.

READING

1 REMEMBER AND CHECK Complete the sentences with the missing words. Then look at the newsletter on page 49 of the Student's Book and check your answers.

0 The article is about a school g _lee_____ club.

1 People s_____ in these clubs.

2 Mrs. Hernandez is a m_____ teacher.

3 They sing songs from m_____ .

4 They perform c_____ in front of the rest of the school three times a year.

5 The club is a good way to make f_____ .

6 The club is in the school a_____ .

7 They meet on Tuesdays and F_____ .

2 Look at the pictures and read the messages. What rooms are these people in? What club are they in?

1 _____

2 _____

3 _____

4 _____

3 Match the sentences with the correct places (A–D) in the messages.

0 Tell your parents it ends at 5:00 p.m. | C |

1 (and some old songs, too). | |

2 It's great for all students who love gadgets. | |

3 Ask your parents about some of their favorites, and we can add them to the list. | |

Computer games club

Come and practice at all your favorite games. Learn from your friends and show them what you know. Mrs. Stephens also shows you how to make your own simple games.
A _____

Grades 7 and 8 – Tuesday, lunchtime, Room 4

• Dance club •

Join Mr. Roberts for an hour of exercise and have lots of fun at the same time. Learn how to dance to all today's best hip hop songs B _____ And it's not just for students at the school – anyone is welcome!'

All grades – Wednesday, lunchtime, in the school gym

Homework club

Don't do all of your homework after school or on weekends. Come to Homework club and do it before you go home. When you get home after school you can have fun! C _____ There's always a teacher here to help you if you have a problem.

All grades – Every day after school, Room 8

Movie club

Watch classic movies from the 1980s and 1990s E.T., Toy Story, Jurassic Park, etc. Then talk about them with Ms. Owens and other students.
D _____ Bring your own popcorn!

Grades 9–11, Thursdays, after school, Room 14

DEVELOPING WRITING

My week

1 Read the text. On which day does Bruno not do any homework?

POSTED: MONDAY 10 APRIL

Bruno's Busy Life

A typical week …

From Monday to Friday, I go to school from 9 a.m. to 3 p.m. every day. But my day doesn't finish then!

After school on Mondays I have piano lessons from 4 p.m. to 5 p.m. In the evenings I do my homework.

On Tuesdays and Thursdays I have tennis lessons from 4 p.m. to 6 p.m. In the evenings I do my homework.

On Wednesday afternoons I go to Dance Club from 3 p.m. to 4 p.m. And in the evenings? Yeah, I do my homework.

On Fridays I do my homework after school! I go to Glee Club in the evenings. It ends at 9 p.m.

On Saturdays I do things with Mom and Dad. We go shopping or visit Grandma. My dad sometimes takes me to watch soccer games.

On Sundays I sleep! Oh, and then I do some homework.

2 Complete the sentences with the correct prepositions. Use the text in Exercise 1 to help you.

1 I have tennis _____ Tuesdays and Thursdays. I play _____ 4:00 p.m. _____ 6:00 p.m.

2 _____ Wednesday afternoons I have a Dance Club. It starts _____ 3:00 p.m. and ends _____ 4:00 p.m.

3 _____ Monday to Friday I go to school.

3 Match the parts of the phrases. Then check your answers in the text in Exercise 1.

1 do ☐
2 go ☐
3 have ☐

a a tennis lesson
b to Dance Club / shopping
c homework

4 Think about your life. Use the questions to make notes about the things you do.

What do you do in the day?

_____

What do you do in the evening?

_____

What do you do on the weekend?

_____

5 Use your notes to complete the text so it is true for you.

A typical week …

From Monday to Friday, I go to school _____ every day! But my day doesn't finish then.
After school on Mondays I _____ .
In the evenings _____ .
On Tuesdays _____ .
In the evenings I _____ .
On Wednesdays _____ .
In the evenings I _____ .
On Thursdays _____ .
In the evenings I _____ .
On Fridays _____ .
In the evenings I _____ .
On Saturdays _____ .
On Sundays _____ .

LISTENING

1 🔊24 **Listen to the dialogue and put the events in order.**

☐	a	Kim feels better.
☐	b	Kim tells her mom about the singing.
☐	c	Kim tells her mom the name of the song.
☐	d	Kim tells her mom the name of the play.
1	e	Kim is unhappy.
☐	f	Mom starts playing the piano.

2 🔊24 **Listen again and correct the sentences.**

0 Kim is on the school tennis team.

 Kim is in the school play.

1 Kim likes acting and singing.

 _____

2 Kim thinks she's a good singer.

 _____

3 The song is from *The Lion King*.

 _____

4 Mom is a good pianist.

 _____

DIALOGUE

Complete the dialogue with the phrases in the list.

don't worry | here to help you | No problem
You can do this | ~~You're great~~

KIM   Yes, my character is Elsa! She sings a lot in the play. And I'm a terrible singer.

MOM   You aren't. ⁰*You're great* . Just like me.

KIM   Really?

MOM   Yes, really. Come on. ¹_____ .

KIM   I can?

MOM   Yes, you can. And I'm ²_____ .

KIM   You are?

MOM   Yes, ³_____ . Now what's the song?

KIM   It's "Let it Go" from the movie.

MOM   ⁴_____ . Come with me to the piano.

2 **Look at the picture and write a short dialogue. Use the phrases from Exercise 1.**

_____

_____

_____

_____

_____

PHRASES FOR FLUENCY SB page 55

1 **Match the sentences.**

0	What's wrong?	d
1	I have an idea.	☐
2	Ana, do you want to be on the school tennis team?	☐
3	I don't want to play soccer.	☐

a Really. What is it?

b No way!

c Oh, come on. We really need you.

d I feel a little sick.

2 **Use two of the pairs of sentences in Exercise 1 to complete the dialogues.**

Dialogue 1

JORGE   _____

SARA   _____

JORGE   But I hate soccer. And I'm terrible at it.

SARA   No, you're not. You're great.

Dialogue 2

ABBY   I'm sorry, Max. I don't really want to go shopping.

MAX   _____

ABBY   _____

MAX   Oh, no. Let's get you a glass of water.

3 **Use the other two pairs of sentences in Exercise 1 to make your own dialogues.**

Sum it up

1 This is Lucy's calendar. Make sentences about her week.

MONDAY	shopping
TUESDAY	dance
WEDNESDAY	friends
THURSDAY	computer games
FRIDAY	homework
SATURDAY	music
SUNDAY	sleep!

0   *On Monday she goes shopping.*

1   _____

2   _____

3   _____

4   _____

5   _____

2 Use the code to figure out the message.

Decoded message:

For my birthday I want a computer and a

_____

games console. I don't want a camera.

_____

I have one.

_____

CODE

♋ = a	♌ = b	♏ = c	♎ = d
♏ = e	✗ = f	♑ = g	≈ = h
♓ = i	⚳ = j	& = k	● = l
○ = m	■ = n	□ = o	▢ = p
◻ = q	☐ = r	£ = s	¤ = t
◆ = u	❖ = v	◆ = w	⊠ = x
⊡ = y	⌘ = z		

3 What do you want? Use the code to write your own message.

_____

_____

_____

GRAMMAR

have (affirmative and negative)
SB page 58

1 ★ ☆ ☆ (Circle) the correct options.

0 I *has /* (*have*) a new friend.

1 My friend Sam *has / have* a tablet.

2 Jenny *has / have* a big family.

3 We *has / have* a cat.

4 All of my friends *has / have* bikes.

2 ★ ★ ☆ Look at the table and complete the sentences.

has / doesn't have	Skye	Tim	Dylan	Emily
smartphone	✓	✗	✓	✗
laptop	✗	✗	✗	✗
bike	✓	✗	✓	✓
TV	✗	✓	✗	✗
dog	✓	✓	✓	✓

0 Tim _____doesn't have_____ a smartphone.

1 Skye _____ a laptop or a TV.

2 Dylan and Emily _____ a bike.

3 Tim _____ a TV.

4 All of them _____ a dog.

5 Tim and Dylan _____ a laptop.

3 ★ ★ ★ Write sentences so they are true for you. Use *have* or *don't have* and the phrases in the list.

a big family | a new phone number
a new smartphone | a sister | a tablet
black hair | brown eyes | three brothers

1 _____

2 _____

3 _____

4 _____

5 _____

6 _____

7 _____

8 _____

4 ★ ★ ★ Write sentences under the pictures. Use the phrases in the list and *have* or *has*.

a shaved head | long curly hair
long straight hair | short curly hair

have (questions) SB page 59

5 ★ ☆ ☆ (Circle) the correct options.

1 A *Does /* (*Do*) you have a TV in your bedroom?

 B No, I *don't / doesn't*. But my brother has one.

2 A *Does / Do* Katy have a friendship band?

 B No, she *don't / doesn't*. She doesn't like them.

3 A *Do / Does* Jake and Andy have new cell phones?

 B No, they *don't / doesn't*. But I *have / has* one.

4 A *Do / Does* you have lots of songs on your phone?

 B Yes, I *do / does*. I have thousands. I listen to music all the time.

5 A *Do / Does* you have bikes?

 B Yes, we *do / does*. We both have bikes. We ride to school every day.

6 A *Do / Does* Simon have a sister?

 B No, he *don't / doesn't*. But he has a brother.

6 ★★ ☆ Complete the dialogue with the correct form of *have*.

JANE   0 ___*Does*___ your mom _____ brown hair?

MARCUS   No, she 1_____ . She 2_____ black hair.

JANE   3_____ she _____ blue eyes?

MARCUS   No, she 4_____ . She 5_____ green eyes.

JANE   6_____ she _____ a daughter?

MARCUS   No, she 7_____ . She 8_____ one son – me!

7 ★★★ Complete the dialogue about a member of your family.

FRIEND   Does he/she have green eyes?
YOU   _____

FRIEND   Does he/she have a big family?
YOU   _____

FRIEND   Does he/she have a car?
YOU   _____

FRIEND   Does he/she have a dog?
YOU   _____

FRIEND   Does he/she have a smartphone?
YOU   _____

Count and noncount nouns   SB page 59

8 ★ ☆ ☆ Write C (count) or N (noncount).

0	chair	C		5	time	
1	nose			6	work	
2	hair			7	hospital	
3	fun			8	name	
4	friend			9	teacher	

9 ★★ ☆ Circle the correct options.

0   It's the weekend. Let's have *a* / *some* fun.

1   I have *a* / *some* sandwiches. Let's eat one.

2   Let's listen to *a* / *some* music on your smartphone.

3   Marie has *a* / *some* red bike.

4   I have *a* / *some* money. Let's buy an ice cream.

5   He has *a* / *some* hobby – painting!

6   My dad has *a* / *some* work to do.

7   Murat doesn't have *an* / *some* apple. He has *a* / *some* banana.

10 ★★ ☆ Complete the dialogues with *a*, *an*, or *some*.

1   A   Would you like ___*some*___ ice cream?
     B   No, thanks. I have _____ apple.

2   A   Do you have _____ hobby?
     B   Yes, I do. I sing in a band.

3   A   Do you have _____ best friend?
     B   Yes, I do. Her name's Zeynep.

4   A   I have _____ money from my mom.
     B   Me, too!
     A   Cool! Let's buy _____ candy.

5   A   I don't have a pen.
     B   Oh, I have _____ . I have blue, black, and red. Is that OK?
     A   Yes, perfect!

GET IT RIGHT!
Count and noncount nouns

We add *-s* to the end of count nouns to make them plural, but not to noncount nouns.

✓ *I have a lot of **friends**.*

✗ *I have a lot of friend.*

✓ *I drink a lot of **water**.*

✗ *I drink a lot of waters.*

Circle the correct options.

0   How many *pen* / *pens* does he have?

1   I listen to *musics* / *music* in my bedroom.

2   They have a lot of *hobby* / *hobbies*.

3   Do you have enough *money* / *moneys* for your lunch?

4   Math class is OK, but I don't like the *homework* / *homeworks*. It isn't always fun.

5   Her brother has two *phone* / *phones*.

6   This street has a lot of *store* / *stores*.

VOCABULARY

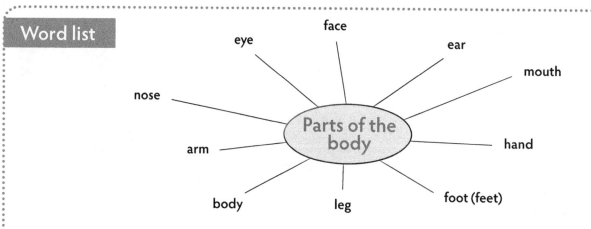

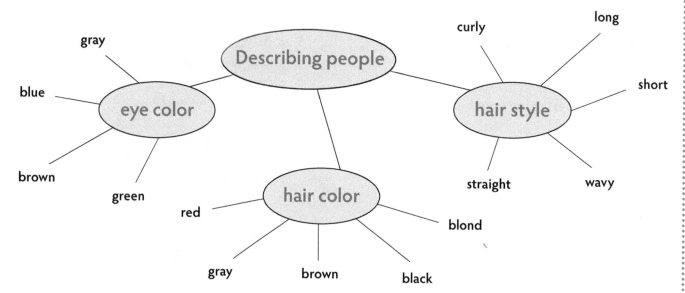

Key words in context

doctor	When I'm sick, I see a **doctor**.
good-looking	Brad has black hair and blue eyes. He's very **good-looking**.
kiss	When we greet a friend in my country, we **kiss** three times on the cheeks.
nurse	My mom is a **nurse** at the hospital.
shaved	My dad doesn't have any hair. He has a **shaved** head.
surprise	I have a gift for Jane. It's a **surprise**.
tradition	I always eat cake on my birthday. It's a **tradition**.

Parts of the body SB page 58

1 ★☆☆ Complete the crossword.

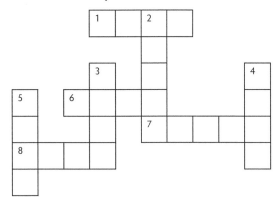

ACROSS

1 You reach with your _____.
6 You kick with your _____.
7 You hold with your _____.
8 You hear with your _____.

DOWN

2 You eat with your _____.
3 You walk with your _____.
4 You smell with your _____.
5 You see with your _____.

Describing people (1) SB page 60

2 ★★☆ Circle the correct options.

0 His hair isn't curly. It's *wavy* / *brown*.
1 She has *short* / *blond* red hair.
2 Her eyes are *straight* / *green*.
3 My mother always wears her hair *straight* / *brown* for work.
4 The old man has gray *curly* / *hair*.
5 His hair *color* / *style* is black.

Describing people (2) SB page 61

3 ★☆☆ Complete the words with *a, e, i, o,* or *u*.

0 m u s t a c h e
1 g l _ s s _ s
2 t _ l l
3 b _ _ r d
4 s m _ l _
5 _ _ r r _ n g s
6 s h _ r t

4 ★★☆ Match the words to the pictures. Write 1–6 in the boxes.

1 beard | 2 earrings | 3 glasses | 4 gray
5 mustache | 6 wavy

5 ★★★ Look at the picture and write the names of the people.

0 She has earrings.   *Seline*
1 He has a very big mustache.   _____
2 She has a lovely smile.   _____
3 He has a very long beard.   _____
4 She wears glasses.   _____

6 ★★★ Write one more sentence about each person in Exercise 4.

1 _____
2 _____
3 _____
4 _____

Pronunciation

The /eɪ/ vowel sound

Go to page 119.

READING

1 REMEMBER AND CHECK **Mark the sentences T (true) or F (false). Then look at the article on page 57 of the Student's Book and check your answers.**

0 Delaney Clements is 12.   [F]

1 Delaney has long curly hair and blue eyes.   [ ]

2 She loves sports.   [ ]

3 Kamryn is her best friend.   [ ]

4 Delaney has cancer.   [ ]

5 Delaney shaves her head.   [ ]

2 **Read the two dialogues about friendship and answer the questions.**

1 Who has green eyes?   _____

2 Who wears glasses?   _____

TANIA	Who is your best friend?
CLARA	Sarah is my best friend.
TANIA	What does she look like?
CLARA	She's very pretty. She has long curly black hair and brown eyes. She wears glasses, and she has a friendly smile.
TANIA	What's she like?
CLARA	She's very smart and very nice. She likes drawing and making things. I like making things, too. We have the same hobbies. That's important, I think.
TANIA	Why is she a good friend?
CLARA	Friends share things with you. Sarah shares everything with me. She shares her chocolate with me and her clothes with me. She's a very special friend.

TANIA	Who is your best friend?
SAM	Murat is my best friend.
TANIA	What does he look like?
SAM	He's tall and has short straight brown hair and green eyes. He has a friendly smile, and he laughs a lot. We laugh a lot together. We like the same things.
TANIA	What's he like?
SAM	He's funny and tells good jokes. He's very good at sports, and he likes basketball. I like basketball, too. We like the same team. That's important, I think.
TANIA	Why is he a good friend?
SAM	Friends listen to you. Murat always listens to me. Sometimes I have a problem, and he helps me. He's a great friend.

3 **Read the dialogues again and answer the questions.**

1 What color is Sarah's hair?   _____

2 What color is Murat's hair?   _____

3 Who likes basketball?   _____

4 Who likes drawing?   _____

5 What do Murat and Sam like?   _____

6 What does Sarah share with Clara?   _____

4 **Who says these phrases about friendship? Write C (Clara) or S (Sam).**

A good friend …

1 [ ] shares things with you.

2 [ ] likes the same team.

3 [ ] helps you.

4 [ ] has the same hobbies.

5 [ ] tells you jokes.

6 [ ] listens to you.

DEVELOPING WRITING

Describing people in a story

1 Read about a singer from a story.
Mark the sentences T (true) or F (false).

1 He's short. ☐
2 He wears glasses. ☐
3 He has a mustache. ☐
4 He doesn't have a beard. ☐
5 He doesn't like tennis. ☐

In my story, there's a singer. He's in a boy band. He's very tall. He has short black hair and blue eyes, and he wears glasses. He has a short beard. I think he's very good-looking. He's very active. He likes soccer and swimming, but he doesn't like tennis. He's very friendly. Look! He has a big smile. I think he's cool.

2 Think of a person from a story. He/She can be a singer, a sportsperson, an actor/actress, a prince/ princess, etc. Choose the adjectives that describe him or her.

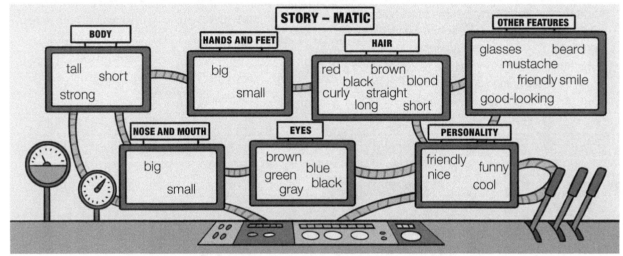

STORY – MATIC

BODY
tall short strong

HANDS AND FEET
big small

HAIR
red brown black blond curly straight long short

OTHER FEATURES
glasses beard mustache friendly smile good-looking

NOSE AND MOUTH
big small

EYES
brown green blue gray black

PERSONALITY
friendly nice funny cool

3 Write notes about your story person. Use the questions to help you.

What does she/he look like? (hair, eyes, other features) _____

_____

Personality _____

Likes / dislikes _____

_____

4 Use your notes to complete the text about your story person.

In my story, there is a/an _____ .
She/He is _____ . She/He has
_____ and _____ .
She/He has _____ and
_____ . And what about his/her
personality? She/He is _____
and _____ . She/He likes
_____ , but she/he doesn't like
_____ .

I like him/her very much.

> ### Writing tip: adjectives to describe people
>
> • She/He is *tall* / *short*.
> • She/He has *long* / *black* / *curly* hair.
> • She/He has *brown* / *blue* / *green* eyes.
> • She/He has a *black* / *gray* / *brown* / *long* / *short* *mustache* / *beard*.
> • She/He is *nice* / *friendly*.

LISTENING

1 🔊 27 **Listen to the dialogues and number the places in the order you hear them.**

a ☐ the park

b ☐ a hospital

c ☐ a party

2 🔊 27 **Listen again and (circle) the correct options.**

1 Martin is *tall / short* and he has short, curly, *brown / black* hair. He has a *mustache / friendship band* and he wears *glasses / earrings*.

2 Rajaa has a *dog / bike* with her. Rajaa is *short / tall* and she has long, curly, *brown / black* hair. She has *brown / blue* eyes and she always wears *glasses / earrings*. She's very *funny / friendly*.

3 The nurse is *tall / short* and she has *short / long* hair. It's *black / blond* and it's *curly / straight*. She has *brown / green* eyes and she's very *popular / pretty*.

DIALOGUE

Put the dialogue in order.

☐	POLICE OFFICER	And what's your daughter's name?
☐	POLICE OFFICER	And what color eyes does she have?
1	POLICE OFFICER	What's your name?
☐	POLICE OFFICER	Thank you, Mrs. Jones.
☐	POLICE OFFICER	OK, first, what color hair does she have?
☐	POLICE OFFICER	Is it long or short?
☐	MRS. JONES	She has brown hair.
☐	MRS. JONES	My name's Sarah Jones.
☐	MRS. JONES	She has green eyes, and she wears glasses.
☐	MRS. JONES	It's Emma.
☐	MRS. JONES	It's short and curly.

■ TRAIN TO THiNK ■

Attention to detail

Find the five differences and write sentences.

Picture 1

Picture 2

0 *In picture 1, the man has glasses.*
  In picture 2, he doesn't have glasses.

1 _____

2 _____

3 _____

4 _____

Punctuation (getting apostrophes right)

Writing tip

When writing in English, it's sometimes easy to make mistakes with apostrophes ('). It's important to know when to use them and when not to use them.

- We use apostrophes to show missing letters in short forms, for example:

  He is … → He's …

  She does not have … → She doesn't have …

- Be careful not to confuse apostrophes for the short form of *be* and *have* with apostrophes to show possession:

  My mom doesn't have curly hair. (short form)

  My mom's name is Helen. (possession)

1 Complete the *Apostrophe Challenge*. Write the short forms.

I think I can complete the *Apostrophe Challenge* in _____ seconds.

I am	0	*I'm*
It is	1	
You are	2	
He is not	3	
They are not	4	
She does not have	5	
I do not have	6	
We do not have	7	
He does not have	8	
You do not have	9	

My time: _____ seconds.

2 Read the text. Put apostrophes in the correct places.

My best <u>friends</u>' name is Miranda. Shes 12 years old, and shes in the same class as me. Mirandas hair is short, brown, and curly. She wears glasses and shes very pretty. Shes smart and shes good at sports. Mirandas brother and sister are 8 and 10. They dont wear glasses. Theyre short and have brown curly hair, too. Mirandas cat is black and white, and its names Suky. Its a great cat.

3 Write a paragraph about one of these people. Use the questions in the box to help you.

a your best friend

b a family member

c your favorite actor or singer

- What's her/his name?
- How old is she/he?
- What does she/he look like?

CONSOLIDATION

LISTENING

1 🔊28 **Listen to three dialogues and (circle) the correct answers (A, B, or C).**

1   Jonathan has a problem with his …
    A   arm.   B   hand.   C   leg.
2   Maddy is …
    A   nice.   B   short.   C   tall.
3   How many friends does the boy have?
    A   about fifty   B   about fifteen   C   about five

2 🔊28 **Listen again and answer the questions.**

1   What does Jonathan want to do today?

2   What does the girl tell him to do?

3   Does Mike know Maddy?

4   What does Mike want Samantha to say to Maddy?

5   When does the boy come to this place?

6   What color is Steve's hair?

GRAMMAR

3 (Circle) **the correct options.**

TOM   Hi, Joanna. How are you? It's nice to see you here.

JOANNA   Hi, Tom. Well, I ¹*come always / always come* to the mall on Saturdays.

JASON   Oh, right. ²*I'm never / I never am* downtown on Saturdays. But it's different today because ³*I have / I'm have* some money.

JOANNA   Great. ⁴*How much / How many* money do you have, then?

TOM $75.00. I ⁵*don't know / know not* what I want to buy, though. Maybe some clothes, or … .

JOANNA   That's a great idea. I love clothes. I ⁶*buy / buys* clothes every month.

TOM   Really? So, do ⁷*you do / you have* lots of clothes at home?

JOANNA   Oh, yeah.

TOM   OK, well I'm not very good at buying clothes. Can you help me? Do you have ⁸*a / some* time to come with me?

JOANNA   Of course. Let's go to this store first – ⁹*it always has / it has always* nice things to buy.

TOM   OK, cool. You know, Joanna, it's great to have ¹⁰*a / some* friend like you!

VOCABULARY

4 **Complete the sentences with the words in the list. There are two extra words.**

do | earrings | e-reader | eyes
hang out | headphones | legs
short | smile | tall

1   I really like listening to music with my
    _____ .
2   Spiders have eight _____ .
3   I like Susannah. She's always happy and she has a nice _____ .
4   These are my new _____ . Do you like them?
5   I don't buy books any more. I have an _____ .
6   She's good at basketball because she's very _____ .
7   I only _____ my homework on Sundays – never on Saturdays!
8   On Sundays I always _____ with my friends.

5 **Complete the words.**

1   My favorite day of the week is F _ _ _ _ _ _ .
2   I use my new t _ _ _ _ _ _ every day to check my emails and things.
3   Her hair isn't straight. It's c _ _ _ _ _ .
4   Let's go out on W _ _ _ _ _ _ _ _ evening – to the movies, maybe?
5   My grandfather has a b _ _ _ _ and a mustache.
6   His eyes aren't very good. He wears g _ _ _ _ _ _ _ all the time.
7   Do you want to go s _ _ _ _ _ _ _ _ downtown tomorrow morning?
8   Raise your h _ _ _ if you know the answer.

DIALOGUE

6 **Complete the dialogue with the words in the list.**

always | an idea | don't have | listen to | never | on | play | tablet | way | wrong

PAUL   Hey, Jen. You don't seem very happy. What's ¹_____ ?

JEN   Hi, Paul. I'm OK. It's nothing.

PAUL   Come ²_____ . Tell me. Is there a problem?

JEN   No, not really. I really want to ³_____ my new computer games tonight, but I ⁴_____ anyone to play with.

PAUL   OK. Listen. I have ⁵_____ . Let's ask Jake to come over to my place. Then we can all play some games together.

JEN   No ⁶_____ ! I don't like Jake at all. He ⁷_____ says anything nice to me. He's ⁸_____ mean to me. He called me "stupid" in class yesterday. Remember that?

PAUL   Oh, right, OK, so forget Jake. Let's you and me play, then. I'm not very good, but …

JEN   Oh, yes, please. That's great, Paul. Thank you. So – can we use your laptop?

PAUL   Sorry, Jen, I don't have a laptop. But I have a ⁹_____ . Is that OK?

JEN   Yes, I think so. And we can ¹⁰_____ music at the same time, too.

PAUL   Sure, let's do it. See you tonight at 7. OK?

READING

7 **Read this text about gadgets and (circle) the correct answers (A or B).**

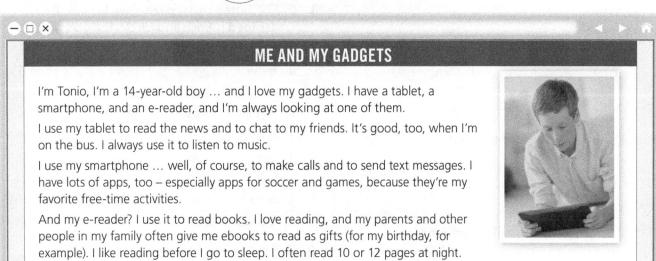

ME AND MY GADGETS

I'm Tonio, I'm a 14-year-old boy … and I love my gadgets. I have a tablet, a smartphone, and an e-reader, and I'm always looking at one of them.

I use my tablet to read the news and to chat to my friends. It's good, too, when I'm on the bus. I always use it to listen to music.

I use my smartphone … well, of course, to make calls and to send text messages. I have lots of apps, too – especially apps for soccer and games, because they're my favorite free-time activities.

And my e-reader? I use it to read books. I love reading, and my parents and other people in my family often give me ebooks to read as gifts (for my birthday, for example). I like reading before I go to sleep. I often read 10 or 12 pages at night.

1   Tonio has …
    A   three gadgets.
    B   four gadgets.

2   He listens to music on …
    A   his smartphone.
    B   his tablet.

3   Tonio uses his smartphone to …
    A   check the weather.
    B   talk to his friends.

4   People in Tonio's family often give him …
    A   ebooks for his reader.
    B   pages from books to read at night.

WRITING

8 **Write a paragraph about your gadgets. Use the questions to help you. Write 35–50 words.**

- What gadgets do you have?
- What do you use them for?
- When / How often do you use them?
- What gadgets do you want?

PRONUNCIATION

UNIT 1
/h/ or /w/ in question words

1 Look at the question words. Two of them start with the /h/ sound and the others start with the /w/ sound. Write /h/ or /w/ next to the words.

0	Why	_/w/_
1	How	
2	Where	
3	Who	
4	What	
5	When	

2 ◖🔊 10 Listen, check, and repeat.

3 Match the words that sound the same.

0	Why		a	now
1	How		b	but
2	Where		c	chair
3	Who		d	then
4	What		e	I
5	When		f	you

4 ◖🔊 11 Listen, check, and repeat.

UNIT 2
Vowel sounds: adjectives

1 ◖🔊 13 Listen and repeat the adjectives.

angry	awful	bored	busy
friendly	funny	happy	hot
hungry	sad	thirsty	worried

2 Complete the table with the words in Exercise 1.

a (cat)	e (get)	i (six)	o (not)
0 _that_	3	4	5
1			6
2			

u (bus)	or (for)	ir (bird)	
7	9	11	
8	10		

3 ◖🔊 14 Listen, check, and repeat.

UNIT 3
this / that / these / those

1 ◖🔊 17 Listen and repeat. Then look at the underlined sounds and (circle) the odd sound out.

0	th<u>o</u>se	g<u>o</u>	h<u>o</u>me	(b<u>o</u>red)
1	th<u>a</u>t	s<u>a</u>d	l<u>a</u>te	h<u>a</u>ve
2	th<u>e</u>m	th<u>e</u>se	pl<u>ea</u>se	m<u>ee</u>t
3	g<u>i</u>ve	l<u>i</u>ke	th<u>i</u>s	s<u>i</u>ng
4	h<u>o</u>t	c<u>o</u>ld	kn<u>ow</u>	th<u>o</u>se
5	w<u>i</u>fe	th<u>i</u>s	n<u>i</u>ce	exc<u>i</u>ting
6	th<u>e</u>se	sh<u>e</u>	g<u>e</u>t	w<u>e</u>
7	f<u>a</u>mous	th<u>a</u>t	f<u>a</u>mily	h<u>a</u>ppy

2 ◖🔊 17 Listen again, check, and repeat.

UNIT 4
Word stress in numbers

1 ◀)19 **Listen to the words and write them in the correct column according to the stress.**

~~eighteen~~ | ~~eighty~~ | forty | fourteen | nineteen
ninety | sixteen | sixty | thirty | thirteen

oO	Oo
eighteen	*eighty*

2 ◀)19 **Listen again, check, and repeat.**

UNIT 5
Simple present verbs: third person

1 **Complete the table with the correct simple present third person singular form of the verbs in the list.**

~~catch~~ | ~~cook~~ | choose | dance | help | look
sing | teach | walk | wash | watch | wish | work

One syllable	Two syllables
cooks	*catches*

2 ◀)23 **Listen, check, and repeat.**

UNIT 6
The /eɪ/ vowel sound

1 ◀)25 **Listen to these words. They all contain the /eɪ/ sound. <u>Underline</u> the sound in each word.**

0   br<u>ea</u>k

0   <u>ei</u>ght

0   f<u>a</u>ce

1   great

2   gray

3   make

4   rainy

5   say

6   straight

7   take

8   they

9   waiter

2 **Complete the sentences with the words in Exercise 1.**

0   How do you _____*say*_____ that word in English?

1   Is your grandmother the woman with the wavy _____ hair?

2   Let's _____ Clara a friendship band for her birthday!

3   My little sister is _____ years old.

4   These are my friends. _____ like playing soccer with me.

5   It's _____ today. Let's go to the movies.

6   My father's a _____ at that restaurant.

7   I brush my teeth and wash my _____ every morning.

8   I like playing tennis. It's a _____ game!

9   Can you _____ this book to your teacher? Thank you.

10   My hair's _____ but my best friend's hair is curly.

11   Put your books away. It's time for a _____ .

3 ◀)26 **Listen, check, and repeat.**

GRAMMAR REFERENCE

UNIT 1
Question words

1 Questions that begin with *Who* ask about a person or people.

Who is he?
He's the new teacher.

2 Questions that begin with *What* ask about a thing or things.

What's that?
It's a mobile phone.

3 Questions that begin with *When* ask about a time, day, year, etc.

When's the baseball game?
It's at three o'clock.

4 Questions that begin with *Where* ask about a place.

Where's Xian?
It's in China.

5 Questions that begin with *Why* ask for a reason.

Why are you here?
Because I want to see you.

6 Questions that begin with *How old* ask about age.

How old is she?
She's sixteen.

The verb *be*

1 The simple present of *be*:

Singular	Plural
I am	we are
you are	you are
he/she/it is	they are

2 In speaking and informal writing we use contracted (short) forms.

I'm, you're, he's, she's, it's, we're, they're

I'm from Merida.
She's late.
We're hungry.

UNIT 2
be (negative: singular, and plural)
We make the verb *be* negative by adding *not*.

Singular	Plural
I **am not** (I**'m not**)	we **are not** (we **aren't**)
you **are not** (you **aren't**)	you **are not** (you **aren't**)
he/she/it **is not** (he/she/it **isn't**)	they **are not** (they **aren't**)

I'm not Brazilian. I'm Portuguese.
He isn't late. He's early!
They aren't from Spain. They're from Mexico.

be (questions and short answers)

To make questions with *be*, we put the verb before the subject. We make short answers with *Yes* or *No* + subject + the verb *be*. We don't use contracted forms in affirmative short answers (NOT: *Yes, you're.*)

Am I late?	Yes, you are. / No, you aren't.
Are you American?	Yes, I am. / No, I'm not.
Is he a singer?	Yes, he is. / No, he isn't.
Is she from Japan?	Yes, she is. / No, she isn't.
Is this answer right?	Yes, it is / No, it isn't.
Are we ready?	Yes, we are. / No, we aren't.
Are they Colombian?	Yes, they are. / No, they aren't.

Object pronouns

1 Object pronouns come after a verb. We use them instead of nouns.

I like the movie. I like it.
I love my sister. I love her.
They want to see you and me. They want to see us.
I like the girls at my school. I like them.

2 The object pronouns are:

Subject	I	you	he	she	it	we	they
Object	me	you	him	her	it	us	them

UNIT 3
Possessive 's

1 We use *'s* after a noun to say who something belongs to.

Dad's room
John's car
Sandra's family
the cat's bed
my brother's friend
your sister's school

2 We don't usually say ~~the room of Dad, the car of John~~, etc.

Possessive adjectives

1 We use possessive adjectives before a noun to say who something belongs to.

My name's Joanne.
Is this your pen?
He's my brother. I'm his sister.
She's nice. I like her smile!
The cat isn't in its bed.
We love our house.
Are the students in their classroom?

2 The possessive adjectives are:

Subject pronoun	I	you	he	she	it	we	they
Possessive adjective	my	your	his	her	its	our	their

this / that / these / those

1 We use *this* or *these* to talk about things that are close to us. We use *that* or *those* to point out things that are not close to us, or are close to other people.

Look at this photo – it's my sister under the tree.
These oranges aren't very good.
That store is a really good place to buy clothes.
We don't like those boys.

2 We use *this* or *that* with a singular noun. We use *these* or *those* with plural nouns.

this photo   *that* house
these rooms   *those* tables

UNIT 4
there is / there are

1 *There is (There's)* and *There are* are used to say that something exists.

There's a small store on our street.
There are two supermarkets near here.
There are lots of great stores downtown.

2 *There's* is the short form of *There is*. In speaking and informal writing, we usually say *There's*.

3 In affirmative sentences, we use *there's* with a singular noun and *there are* with plural nouns.

There's a cat in the garden.
There's a boy in the café.
There are great stores on this street.

4 In questions and negative sentences, we use *a/an* with a singular noun and *any* with plural nouns.

Is there a bank near here?   *There isn't a bank near here.*
Are there any restaurants here?   *There aren't any restaurants here.*

some / any

1 We use *some* and *any* with plural nouns.

There are some good movies on TV tonight.
There aren't any games on my tablet.

2 We use *some* in affirmative sentences. We use *any* in negative sentences and questions.

There are some big trees in the park.
There aren't any places to play sports here.
Are there any good bookstores in the town?

Imperatives

1 We use the imperative to tell someone to do something, or not to do something.

Come here!
Don't open the door!

2 The affirmative imperative is the same as the base form of the verb.

Turn right.
Open the window, please.

3 The negative imperative is formed with *Don't* and the base form of the verb.

Don't listen to him – he's wrong!
Don't open the window – it's cold in here.

UNIT 5
Simple present

1 The simple present is used to talk about things that happen regularly or are usually true.

I go to school at eight o'clock every day.
She watches TV after school.
We play the piano.
They love chocolate.

2 The simple present is usually the same as the base form, but we add *-s* with 3rd person singular (*he/she/it*).

I like pizza.   *He likes pizza.*
They live in Dallas.   *She lives in Argentina.*

3 If the verb ends with *o, sh, ch, ss, z,* or *x*, we add *-es*.

go – he goes   *finish – it finishes*   *catch – she catches*
miss – it misses   *fix – he fixes*

4 If the verb ends with a consonant + -*y*, the *y* changes to *i* and we add -*es*.

carry – it carries   study – he studies   fly – it flies

5 If the verb ends with a vowel + -*y*, it is regular.

buy – she buys   say – he says

Adverbs of frequency

1 Adverbs of frequency tell us *how often* people do things. Adverbs of frequency include:

always	usually	often	sometimes	hardly ever	never

100%   0%

2 Adverbs of frequency come after the verb *be*, but before other verbs.

*I'm **always** hungry in the morning.*
*I **usually eat** breakfast at 7:00.*
*He's **often** tired.*
*He **sometimes goes** to bed early.*
*They're **never** late.*
*They **hardly ever** go on holiday.*

Simple present: negative

The negative of the simple present is formed with *don't* (*do not*) or *doesn't* (*does not*) + base form of the verb.

*I **don't play** tennis.*
*She **doesn't play** the piano.*
*My grandparents **don't live** with us.*
*My brother **doesn't live** with us.*

Simple present: questions

Simple present questions are formed with *Do / Does* + subject + base form of the verb.

Do you like this movie?   *Does Mike like shopping?*
Do I know you?   *Does she know the answer?*
*Do your friends play   *Does your dog like to play*
video games?*   *with balls?*

UNIT 6
have (affirmative and negative)

1 The verb *have/has* is used to talk about things that people own.

*I **have** a bicycle.* (= There is a bicycle and it is my bicycle.)
*He **has** a problem.* (= There is a problem and it is his problem.)

2 We use *have* with *I/you/we/they.* We use *has* with *he/she/it.*

3 The negative form is regular.

*I **don't have** a tablet.*
*This town **doesn't have** a park.*
*They **don't have** a car.*

have (questions)

The question form of *have* is regular. *Do/Does* + subject + *have.* Short answers use *does/do* or *don't/doesn't.*

Do you have my book?   Yes, I **do.**
Does your father have brown hair? Yes, he **does.**
Does the store have any new DVDs? No, it **doesn't.**

Count and noncount nouns

Nouns in English are count or noncount.

1 Count nouns have a singular and a plural form. We can count them. We use *a/an* with the singular nouns. We can use *some* with the plural nouns.

*He has **a house**.*   *He has **two houses**.*
*There's **a picture** on my wall.* *There are **six pictures** on my wall.*
*There's **an orange** in*   *There are **some orange**s in*
the fridge.   *the fridge.*

2 Noncount nouns are always singular. They don't have a plural form. We can't count them. We can use *some* with uncountable nouns.

*I like **music**.*   *Let's listen to **some music**.*
*I like Japanese **food**.*   *Let's eat **some** Japanese **food**.*

3 We don't use *a/an* or numbers with noncount nouns.

NOT ~~a bread~~   ~~an information~~   ~~three works~~

IRREGULAR VERBS

Base form	Simple past
be	was
begin	began
buy	bought
can	could
catch	caught
choose	chose
come	came
do	did
draw	drew
drink	drank
drive	drove
eat	ate
fall	fell
feel	felt
find	found
fly	flew
get	got
give	gave
go	went
have	had
hear	heard
keep	kept
know	knew
leave	left
light	lit

Base form	Simple past
make	made
meet	met
pay	paid
put	put
read /riːd/	read /red/
ride	rode
run	ran
say	said
see	saw
sell	sold
send	sent
sing	sang
sit	sat
sleep	slept
speak	spoke
stand	stood
take	took
teach	taught
tell	told
think	thought
understand	understood
wake	woke
wear	wore
write	wrote

Acknowledgments

The authors and publishers acknowledge the following sources of copyright material and are grateful for the permissions granted. While every effort has been made, it has not always been possible to identify the sources of all the material used or to trace all copyright holders. If any omissions are brought to our notice, we will be happy to include the appropriate acknowledgments on reprinting.

Corpus

Development of this publication has made use of the Cambridge English Corpus (CEC). The CEC is a computer database of contemporary spoken and written English, which currently stands at over one billion words. It includes British English, American English, and other varieties of English. It also includes the Cambridge Learner Corpus, developed in collaboration with Cambridge English Language Assessment. Cambridge University Press has built up the CEC to provide evidence about language use that helps to produce better language teaching materials.

English Profile

This product is informed by the English Vocabulary Profile, built as part of English Profile, a collaborative program designed to enhance the learning, teaching, and assessment of English worldwide. Its main funding partners are Cambridge University Press and Cambridge English Language Assessment and its aim is to create a "profile" for English linked to the Common European Framework of Reference for Languages (CEF). English Profile outcomes, such as the English Vocabulary Profile, will provide detailed information about the language that learners can be expected to demonstrate at each CEF level, offering a clear benchmark for learners' proficiency. For more information, please visit www.englishprofile.org

Cambridge Dictionaries

Cambridge dictionaries are the world's most widely used dictionaries for learners of English. The dictionaries are available in print and online at dictionary.cambridge.org. Copyright © Cambridge University Press, reproduced with permission.

The publishers are grateful to the following for permission to reproduce copyright photographs and material:

T = Top, B = Below, L = Left, R = Right, C = Center, B/G = Background

p. 5 (TL): Peshkova / Getty Images; p. 5 (TL): © Michael Dwyer / Alamy; p. 5 (TL): © Rrrainbow / Alamy; p. 5 (TL): © Zoonar GmbH / Alamy; p. 5 (TL): Foodcollection / Getty Images; p. 5 (TL): CBCK-Christine / Getty Images; p. 5 (TL): © The Picture Pantry / Alamy; p. 5 (TL): fStop Images / Getty Images; p. 5 (TL): © Tetra Images / Alamy; p. 5 (TL): © YAY Media AS / Alamy; p. 5 (TL): vsl / Shutterstock; p. 5 (BL): © Ivan Vdovin / Alamy; p. 5 (BL): © Tom Grundy / Alamy; p. 5 (BL): © Tetra Images / Alamy; p. 5 (BL): © russ witherington / Alamy; p. 5 (BL): © Nadiya Teslyuk / Alamy; p. 6 (TR): Jose Luis Pelaez Inc / Getty Images; p. 6 (BR): © TongRo Images / Alamy; p. 7 (TL): koya79 / Getty Images; p. 7 (TL): ©

Archideaphoto / Alamy; p. 7 (TL): © RTimages / Alamy; p. 7 (TL): Datacraft Co Ltd / Getty Images; p. 7 (TL): © Dmitry Rukhlenko / Alamy; p. 7 (TL): Hemera Technologies / Getty Images; p. 7 (TL): © Anton Starikov / Alamy; p. 7 (TL): © aviv avivbenor / Alamy; p. 7 (BL): © Héctor Sánchez / Alamy; p. 7 (BL): © Zoonar GmbH / Alamy; p. 7 (BR): © Robert Fried / Alamy; p. 7 (BR): Siri Stafford / Getty Images; p. 10 (BL): © Radius Images / Alamy; p. 11 (BL): filipefrazao / Getty Images; p. 11 (BL): © PHOVOIR / Alamy; p. 11 (BL): © wareham.nl (sport) / Alamy; p. 11 (BL): © E.D. Torial / Alamy; p. 11 (BL): © Colin young-wolff / Alamy Stock Photo; p. 11 (BL): STOCK4B/ Getty Images; p. 13 (TR): © wiba / Alamy; p. 13 (TR): © HolgerBurmeister / Alamy; p. 14 (CR): © James Davies / Alamy; p. 14 (CR): AFP / Getty Images; p. 15 (TR): Kali Nine LLC / Getty Images; p. 15 (TR): Kali Nine LLC / Getty Images; p. 15 (TR): omgimages / Getty Images; p. 16 (TL): Laurence Cartwright Photograph/ Getty Images; p. 16 (TL): © Bloomimage/ Corbis; p. 16 (TL): Juanmonino/ Getty Images; p. 16 (TL): © Tetra Images / Alamy; p. 16 (TL): PeopleImages.com / Getty Images; p. 17 (TL): Purestock / Getty Images; p. 17 (TL): Lya_Cattel/ Getty Images; p. 17 (TL): Thierry Levenq / Getty Images; p. 17 (TL): © Horizon Images/Motion / Alamy; p. 19 (TL): Digital Vision / Getty Images; p. 22 (CR): © ZUMA Press, Inc. / Alamy; p. 24 (TL): © age fotostock / Alamy; p. 27 (CL): Image Source / Getty Images; p. 27 (TL): © Katrina Brown / Alamy; p. 27 (TR): Hill Street Studios / Getty Images; p. 31 (CR): © Archideaphoto / Alamy; p. 31 (CR): © Y H Lim / Alamy; p. 31 (CR): Charlie Dean / Getty Images; p. 31 (CR): Christopher Steer / Getty Images; p. 31 (CR): PhotoAlto / Laurence Mouton / Getty Images; p. 31 (CR): Maciej Toporowicz, NYC/ Getty Images; p. 32 (TR): © Eric Audras/Onoky/Corbis; p. 37 (TR): Paul Bradbury / Getty Images; p. 40 (TR): © Image Source / Alamy; p. 41 (TR): © OJO Images Ltd / Alamy; p. 44 (BR): © Danny Smythe / Alamy; p. 44 (BR): flyfloor / Getty Images; p. 44 (BR): satori13/ Getty Images; p. 44 (BR): © Art Directors & TRIP / Alamy; p. 44 (BR): © Y H Lim / Alamy; p. 51 (TR): © Victorio Castellani / Alamy; p. 51 (TR): John Rowley/ Getty Images; p. 54 (TR): Andresr / Shutterstock; p. 54 (TR): © debbiewibowo / RooM the Agency / Corbis; p. 54 (TR): © Beau Lark/Corbis; p. 54 (TR):© Image Source / Corbis; p. 55 (TR): Tetra Images / Getty Images; p. 59 (TR): Luna Vandoorne / Shutterstock; p. 61 (BL): © Radius Images / Alamy; p. 63 (BR): Tetra Images / Getty Images.

Cover photographs by: (L): ©Tim Gainey/Alamy Stock Photo; (R): ©Yuliya Koldovska/Shutterstock.

The publishers are grateful to the following illustrators:

Christos Skaltsas (hyphen) 6, 8 (L), 10, 26, 28, 35 (L), 38, 39 (R), 43, 46, 50, 52, 56, 57, 59, 60 and Zaharias Papadopoulos (hyphen) 8 (R), 12, 16, 20, 35 (TR), 39 (L), 44, 48, 58

The publishers are grateful to the following contributors:

hyphen: editorial, design, and project management; CityVox, LLC: audio recordings; Karen Elliott: Pronunciation sections; Matt Norton: Get it right! exercises